Quarterly Essay

MOMENT OF TRUTH
History and Australia's Future
Mark McKenna

Quarterly Essay is published four times a year by Black Inc., an imprint of Schwartz Publishing Pty Ltd. Publisher: Morry Schwartz.

ISBN 9781760640507 ISSN 1832-0953

Subscriptions – 1 year print & digital
(4 issues): $79.95 within Australia incl. GST.
Outside Australia $119.95. 2 years print & digital
(8 issues): $149.95 within Australia incl. GST.
1 year digital only: $49.95.

Payment may be made by Mastercard or Visa, or by cheque made out to Schwartz Publishing. Payment includes postage and handling.

To subscribe, fill out and post the subscription card or form inside this issue, or subscribe online:

www.quarterlyessay.com
subscribe@blackincbooks.com
Phone: 61 3 9486 0288

Correspondence should be addressed to:

The Editor, Quarterly Essay
Level 1, 221 Drummond Street
Carlton VIC 3053 Australia
Phone: 61 3 9486 0288 / Fax: 61 3 9011 6106
Email: quarterlyessay@blackincbooks.com

Editor: Chris Feik. Management: Caitlin Yates. Publicity: Anna Lensky. Design: Guy Mirabella. Assistant Editor: Kirstie Innes-Will. Production Coordinator: Hanako Smith. Typesetting: Tristan Main.

In memory of Gatjil Djerrkura (1949–2004)
and Inga Clendinnen (1934–2016)

There remains a scar on the face of the country, a birthstain of injustice and exclusion directed against that people who could so easily provide the core of our sense of ourselves as a nation, but who remain on the fringes of the land they once possessed.

Inga Clendinnen, 1999

What Aboriginal people ask is that the modern world now makes the sacrifices necessary to give us a real future. To relax its grip on us. To let us breathe, to let us be free of the determined control exerted on us to make us like you ... Let us be who we are — Aboriginal people in a modern world — and be proud of us. Acknowledge that we have survived the worst that the past has thrown at us, and we are here with our songs, our ceremonies, our land, our language and our people — our full identity. What a gift this is that we can give you, if you choose to accept us in a meaningful way.

Galarrwuy Yunupingu, 2016

We, gathered at the 2017 National Constitutional Convention, coming from all points of the southern sky, make this statement from the heart:

Our Aboriginal and Torres Strait Islander tribes were the first sovereign Nations of the Australian continent and its adjacent islands, and possessed it under our own laws and customs. This our ancestors did, according to the reckoning of our culture, from the Creation, according to the common law from "time immemorial," and according to science more than 60,000 years ago.

This sovereignty is a spiritual notion: the ancestral tie between the land, or "mother nature," and the Aboriginal and Torres Strait Islander peoples who were born therefrom, remain attached thereto, and must one day return thither to be united with our ancestors. This link is the basis of the ownership of the soil, or better, of sovereignty. It has never been ceded or extinguished, and co-exists with the sovereignty of the Crown.

How could it be otherwise? That peoples possessed a land for sixty millennia and this sacred link disappears from world history in merely the last two hundred years?

With substantive constitutional change and structural reform, we believe this ancient sovereignty can shine through as a fuller expression of Australia's nationhood.

Proportionally, we are the most incarcerated people on the planet. We are not an innately criminal people. Our children are aliened from their families at unprecedented rates. This cannot be because we have no love for them. And our youth languish in detention in obscene numbers. They should be our hope for the future. These dimensions of our crisis tell plainly the structural nature of our problem. This is the torment of our powerlessness.

We seek constitutional reforms to empower our people and take a rightful place in our own country. When we have power over our destiny our children will flourish. They will walk in two worlds and their culture will be a gift to their country.

We call for the establishment of a First Nations Voice enshrined in the Constitution.

Makarrata is the culmination of our agenda: *the coming together after a struggle*. It captures our aspirations for a fair and truthful relationship with the people of Australia and a better future for our children based on justice and self-determination.

We seek a Makarrata Commission to supervise a process of agreement-making between governments and First Nations and truth-telling about our history.

In 1967 we were counted, in 2017 we seek to be heard. We leave base camp and start our trek across this vast country. We invite you to walk with us in a movement of the Australian people for a better future.

26 May 2017

MOMENT OF TRUTH

History and Australia's Future

Mark McKenna

Walk across the vast open spaces of Canberra's Parliamentary Triangle and there is more than enough room to reflect on Australia's future. Nature has been ironed out. It's all grass and sky. Standing in the strip between the Tent Embassy and Lake Burley Griffin, the invented nature of the place hits you in the face. And the silence.

It is not only the absence of any acknowledgment of the country's violent foundation that makes the silence palpable, but also 65,000 years of Indigenous occupation. If it were not for the Tent Embassy and the easily missed Reconciliation Place, Indigenous Australia would have no obvious presence within the Parliamentary Triangle. More than a century after federation, Australians still struggle to include Indigenous people in our vision of the nation.

Since the doors of Old Parliament House opened on 9 May 1927, Aboriginal people have beaten a path to Canberra to remind the Commonwealth that their rights and sovereignty have not been extinguished. First in a long line of petitioners were Jimmy Clements and John Noble, two Wiradjuri elders who walked over 150 kilometres from Tumut in southern New South Wales to attend the opening ceremony at

Parliament House in the presence of the Duke and Duchess of York. When it came time for officials and dignitaries to be paraded before the royal couple, Clements insisted on his right to be presented. As Melbourne's *Argus* reported, "an ancient Aborigine, who calls himself King Billy and who claims sovereign rights to the Federal Territory, walked slowly forward alone, and saluted the Duke and Duchess." Clements was eighty years of age. One photograph of him taken that day shows a bearded man sitting in the dust, surrounded by his sleeping dogs, clutching an Australian flag. When he died three months later, a newspaper reported that he was buried in Queanbeyan cemetery, "outside consecrated ground."

Clements walked to Canberra to claim his "sovereign rights" at the very moment the sovereignty of the Crown and the Australian parliament was asserted. One year later, on behalf of the Aborigines Progressive Association, Fred Maynard wrote to the Royal Commission on the Constitution of the Commonwealth to remind the nation's leaders that the constitution and laws that governed the lives of "Aborigines ... were an insult to the intelligence of our people." Since then, the line of petitioners is long, yet their names barely register in the memory of most non-Aboriginal Australians. They include the leaders of the 1967 referendum and the founders of the Tent Embassy, and the authors of both the 1988 Barunga Statement and, of course, the Uluru Statement from the Heart, transmitted from the country's spiritual centre to its political centre – all of them hoping, like the Yirrkala petitioners in 1963, that they would not be "completely ignored" by the Commonwealth government, "as they have been ignored in the past."

If the voice of one Indigenous leader resounds more than any other, it is surely that of Yorta Yorta activist William Cooper. In 1934, Cooper drafted a petition to King George V. The message was unambiguous. Indigenous lands had been "expropriated" by successive Australian governments and their inhabitants' legal status unjustly "denied." He wanted a voice for Aboriginal people and he asked the King that they be granted the power to "propose a member of parliament."

Cooper delivered the petition to the Commonwealth government, led by Joseph Lyons, in September 1937. It carried over 1800 signatures. Two months later, with fellow campaigners Doug Nicholls and William Ferguson, Cooper called for a "Day of Mourning" on Australia Day, 1938, to protest the white man's seizure of their land and to demand full citizenship rights. In March, the Lyons government informed Cooper that it would neither support his demand for parliamentary representation nor forward his petition to King George VI. Incensed by the hypocrisy of a supposedly Christian nation's refusal to accept the equal humanity of Indigenous Australians, Cooper wrote a stinging response to Lyons.

> White men ... claimed that they had "found" a "new" country – Australia. This country was not new, it was already in possession of and inhabited by millions of blacks, who, while unarmed, excepting spears and boomerangs, nevertheless owned the country as their God given heritage ... Every shape and form of murder, yes, mass murder, was used against us and laws were passed and still exist, which no human creature can endure. Our food stuffs have been destroyed, poison and guns have done their work, and now white men's homes have been built on our hunting and camping grounds. Our lives have been wrecked and our happiness ended. Oh! Ye whites! ... How much compensation have we had? How much of our land has been paid for? Not one iota. Again we state that we are the original owners of the country. In spite of force, prestige, or anything else you like, morally the land is ours.

Much of what Cooper said bears a remarkable resemblance to the demands of Indigenous leaders today. He asked for recognition and acknowledgment. He petitioned for a voice in parliament. And he wanted the truth told. At the heart of his campaign was what he called the "horror and fear of extermination" that in one way or another had touched every Aboriginal community in the country.

Yet today, if one scans the monumental landscape of Canberra's Parliamentary Triangle, there is no acknowledgment that such events ever took place. The nation simply rises unencumbered from the ground.

Like every place in Australia, Canberra has its whitefella creation stories. Among them is one told by the "father of Canberra," journalist and NSW MP John Gale. Probably apocryphal, it tells of a day in the late 1850s when Gale, "travelling across country," was helped by a local squatter to cross the flooded Molonglo River. To gain a clearer view of the country, he "rode on to the top of a hill." From there, standing "under a giant kurrajong tree," he gazed out "in delight over a magnificent panorama" and foresaw a new Jerusalem.

"What a site for a city!" he exclaimed. Sixty-three years later, in 1920, "Gale was present to see the Prince of Wales, under the same kurrajong, set one of the foundation stones of the city of Canberra."

Gale's recollection, tailored after Canberra's foundation, was typical of the Biblical narratives that settlers told to sanction their taking up of an "empty" land. Kurrajong Hill, the site of Gale's epiphany, has since been renamed Capital Hill, where Parliament House stands.

For the Ngunnawal, however, Kurrajong Hill was one of several campsites in the Canberra area connected by traditional pathways that saw "local and regional Aboriginal people … come together" for important seasonal ceremonies, like their Bogong festivals that celebrated the arrival of moths in the mountains.

Today, the two histories that coexist on the hill have yet to find a way to meet. And William Cooper's words go unanswered. At a fundamental level, we have failed to see, failed to listen, failed even to hear.

In 2014, "Uncle" Boydie Turner – determined that his grandfather's words be delivered to the house of their original addressee – submitted Cooper's petition to Queen Elizabeth II via Governor-General Sir Peter Cosgrove. It had taken eighty years to arrive. How long before it receives a response?

FROM THE HEART

Yolngu country, August 2017. The annual Garma Festival in northeast Arnhem Land is in its nineteenth year. It is barely three months after the release of the Uluru Statement and only weeks after the Referendum Council's final report, which endorsed the Uluru recommendations, and expectations are high. More than two thousand people have gathered to discuss the central theme of this year's gathering, "*Makarrata*," a Yolngu word for "healing" or "coming together after a struggle." At the heart of *Makarrata* is truth-telling, an elusive habit for much of Australia's history.

Prime Minister Malcolm Turnbull and Opposition leader Bill Shorten have both made the pilgrimage to a place that's invariably described by the media as "remote." Here, way out of their comfort zone, Canberra's elders can appear decidedly ordinary compared to the undeniable stature of their Indigenous counterparts. Like polite visitors from another country, dazed by the heat and the kaleidoscope of theatre and ceremony, they are courteous and attentive, but prone to platitudes. Every year, another Garma holds out the promise that one of them will break the mould.

Official proceedings are dominated by Dr Galarrwuy Yunupingu, leader of the Gumatj clan and a towering figure in the campaign for Indigenous rights. Battling ill-health and recovering from a kidney transplant, he addresses the audience from his wheelchair, reading slowly from a script. Turnbull and Shorten sit in front of him, only metres away. "At Uluru we started a fire," he tells them haltingly, "a fire that we hope burns brighter for Australia." His fellow Indigenous leaders, many of whom have worked for years on committees and consultative groups along the long, tortuous road to recognition, are listening. Yunupingu's incendiary metaphor captures their hope that the Statement from the Heart will receive widespread support. All eyes are on Turnbull and Shorten.

Turnbull begins by congratulating the Referendum Council on its report – the fourth in as many years – and "on reaching an agreement" at Uluru three months earlier. He frames his response as a series of questions and challenges, although his reluctance to embrace the key recommendations from Uluru – a constitutionally enshrined "First Nations voice," which would *advise* parliament on legislation pertaining to Indigenous Australians, and a "Makarrata Commission to supervise a process of agreement-making between governments and First Nations and truth-telling about our history" – is patent. He offers the occasional olive branch – "the answers are not beyond us" – but remains noncommittal. What would this voice "look like," he wonders: "Is our highest aspiration to have Indigenous people outside the parliament providing advice to the parliament, or is it to have as many Indigenous voices elected within our parliament?"

Of course, these aspirations are not mutually exclusive. Lurking just beneath the surface of Turnbull's remarks is the suggestion that the supremacy of parliament is threatened by a First Nations voice.

Turnbull points out that every piece of parliamentary legislation relates to Indigenous Australians. Would the advisory body, he asks, seek to comment on every bill? And what of juvenile justice and other legislation that is the domain of state and territory governments? It is all beginning to sound too hard. Eager to remind Indigenous leaders of his bitter personal experience leading the "Yes" vote in the 1999 republic referendum, he cautions them: "Australians are constitutionally conservative. The bar is surmountable ... but [a double majority of states and voters] is a high bar." Turnbull's argument, which has become conventional wisdom, conflates the voting tendencies of the Australian people with section 128 of the constitution. It is not the people who are necessarily conservative – witness the result of the same-sex marriage survey, which was conducted on the more democratic basis of a simple majority – but the mechanism by which the people vote for constitutional change. The people are more enlightened than their constitution allows them to be.

Shorten's response is both heartening and frustrating. "Labor supports a voice for Aboriginal people in our Constitution," he declares, "we support a declaration by all parliaments, we support a truth-telling commission. We are not confronted by the notion of treaties with our

First Australians." But then comes the rider. Shorten suggests yet another bipartisan parliamentary committee to prepare the recommendations for a referendum on the advisory body.

After so many committees in recent years – Julia Gillard's Expert Panel on recognition (2012), Tony Abbott's Joint Select Committee (2015) and Turnbull and Shorten's Referendum Council (2017) – the mere word is anathema to Pat Anderson, the co-chair of the Referendum Council. Like so many others, she has worked her way through countless dialogues and consultations: the Uluru Statement was the unanimous position to emerge from that lengthy process. Now she is being told that another committee should be convened. Yet another delay. Yet another failure to resolve what needs to be resolved. "They will do anything and everything except talk to us," she says, exasperated.

Worse was to come. On 26 October, the day before the High Court handed down its decision on "the Citizenship Seven," effectively ruling five federal MPs ineligible to sit in parliament, Turnbull released his government's response to the Referendum Council's report. There was no press conference or address to the nation to indicate the importance of the issue. The timing could not have been more cynical. Politicians were preoccupied with their own survival and the deadline for the same-sex marriage survey forms was little more than a week away.

A former Liberal senator and Referendum Council member, Amanda Vanstone, had provided Turnbull with ammunition in her "qualifying statement" in the council's report. Frustrated with what she saw as Uluru's shift away from "symbolic constitutional change," Vanstone was deeply sceptical of the proposed advisory body – the new "can" that Indigenous consultations had put "on the field" – believing it had little chance in a referendum. "The electorate is not all fired up," she remarked, "let alone set alight with enthusiasm." Despite her reservations, Vanstone was respectful of the dialogues and careful not to frame her statement as dissenting. She was still willing to work towards a broadly acceptable "Indigenous voice to parliament."

Turnbull, however, left little room for compromise. He rejected the idea of an Indigenous advisory body unequivocally, announced another joint select committee and shelved the whole question of recognition indefinitely. With any luck, after a few days of negative publicity, the media focus would shift elsewhere. The language of the government's response was emphatic and left no doubt who would be advising whom:

> Our democracy is built on the foundation of all Australian citizens having equal civic rights – all being able to vote for, stand for and serve in either of the two chambers of our national Parliament – the House of Representatives and the Senate. A constitutionally enshrined additional representative assembly for which only Indigenous Australians could vote for or serve in is inconsistent with this fundamental principle. It would inevitably become seen as a third chamber of parliament ... Moreover, the government does not believe such a radical change to our constitution's representative institutions has any realistic prospect of being supported by a majority of Australians in a majority of states ... The Council's proposal for an Indigenous representative assembly, or Voice, is new to the discussion about constitutional change ... The challenge remains to find a constitutional amendment that will succeed, and which does not undermine the universal principles of unity, equality and "one person one vote."

The statement was both deliberately misleading – Turnbull was happy to peddle Barnaby Joyce's earlier lie that the advisory body would act as a third chamber – and wilfully blind to Australia's history. Colonial, state and federal governments had denied Indigenous Australians "equal civic rights" since the late eighteenth century. Now the government threw equality back in their face. No "special treatment." No First Nations (only one nation). No acknowledgment of the long history of profound neglect and interference – we are all equal now.

Although polling suggested – and would continue to suggest over subsequent polls – majority public support for an Indigenous advisory body,

Turnbull claimed to know the result of the referendum in advance. Yet another Australian government was telling Indigenous Australians that it knew what was best for them. The proposal, he insisted, was too "radical" to have any chance of success. Radical? Even Alan Jones – resplendent in his gold jacket and tie on the ABC's *Q&A* – supported the idea. When asked for evidence that the advisory body would "go down in flames" in a referendum, the response of Senator Nigel Scullion, Minister for Indigenous Affairs, was astonishing for its arrogance: "I don't need evidence … we have done a lot of polling, not on this particular matter, but on other matters … [and in any case] evidence is a long string … it's our instincts."

More of the government's instincts were on display when Malcolm Turnbull fronted *Q&A* five days after the same-sex marriage bill was passed in the House of Representatives on 6 December, parliament's final sitting day of the year. Emboldened by the survey result, Turnbull was in a combative mood – the pugnacious barrister in full flight. When audience member and lawyer Teela Reid, who had been part of the dialogues leading to Uluru, pressed him about his misrepresentation of the advisory body as a third chamber with a potential veto over parliament, Turnbull became agitated.

"What's wrong with the [Indigenous] MPs that are in parliament?" he asked, shifting the focus of the discussion, before accusing her of portraying Indigenous MPs as "tokens." Reid didn't take a backward step, telling Turnbull that his rejection of the Council's recommendations had undermined our democracy and that Australia would have to wait for a leader with more "courage." But it was Turnbull who had the last word, suggesting that Reid's support for an Indigenous advisory body was tantamount to being disrespectful of Indigenous MPs: "Aboriginal members of the House and the Senate … are proud first Australians," he declaimed, "powerful voices with 60,000 years of history in our parliament. And I respect them. And I think all Australians should too."

It was galling to watch. Accused by Reid and many others of having no respect, Turnbull turned the argument back on her, claiming the moral high ground for himself and casting Reid as the disrespectful one.

It was a salutary reminder of how difficult it is to raise Indigenous affairs above the partisan fray.

Back in 2013, on the fifth anniversary of the Apology to the Stolen Generations, Prime Minister Julia Gillard and Opposition leader Tony Abbott had led the passage of an "Act of Recognition" through parliament that was "designed to give momentum for constitutional recognition for Indigenous Australians." Indigenous leaders, including Pat Dodson and Lowitja O'Donoghue, looked on from the public gallery as the legislation was passed. Gillard spoke of "the unhealed wound ... at the heart of our nation story," while Abbott painted conservatives and Labor as "partners and collaborators" in the task of recognising Aboriginal people in the nation's "founding charter." Abbott saw the gravity of the occasion, claiming that Australia's failure to recognise Indigenous Australians in the constitution was a "stain" on the nation's soul. Fine words indeed. But what of the fine print? Significantly, Abbott also pointed to the difficulty of agreeing on a future referendum proposal, insisting that recognition had to be achieved "without creating new categories of discrimination." Four years on, Turnbull's rejection of an advisory body rested on exactly the same argument, which is why Abbott, in his new role as the permanently disgruntled gadfly for Warringah, rushed to Facebook to endorse Turnbull's decision.

Indigenous recognition – caught up inevitably in Canberra's internal machinations and power plays – met the same fate as any everyday political proposal. The dream of bipartisanship that had driven Indigenous affairs since 1991, when the Council for Aboriginal Reconciliation was established with the support of all major parties, was well intentioned but politically naive. In the wake of the Turnbull government's response to the Uluru Statement, Noel Pearson was right to argue that the era of bipartisanship is "dead" (if it ever was truly alive from the moment, in the late 1990s, that John Howard attacked the "Aboriginal industry").

By the time Bill Shorten delivered his response to Turnbull's "Closing the Gap" report in parliament in February 2018, it was clear that he agreed with Pearson. "Bipartisanship," said Shorten, did not mean "agreement to do nothing." Shorten's instincts had shifted since Garma. Now he promised that a future Labor government would legislate to create an Indigenous advisory voice to parliament before putting the plan to a referendum. This would allow Australians "lived experience" of the body, he argued, which would lessen the impact of the predictable bevy of scaremongers determined to derail the idea. Labor would work together with the Uluru delegates to "begin the detailed design work" necessary for the body to be legislated.

In response, Turnbull remained unmoved, threatening that if Labor went ahead with its proposal, it would become a "big election issue." Perhaps this is the necessary battle that has to be fought. In the end, concrete reforms, especially those involving constitutional change, have to be won or lost in an adversarial and volatile political environment. Rather than seek full bipartisan support, the task is to secure enough of the political centre to marginalise the rump, whichever party its recalcitrant members might reside in. The circuitous process of the same-sex marriage debate was a case in point.

Indigenous leaders did all they could in the wake of Turnbull's intransigence. They pointed out repeatedly that the way the advisory body would work was left entirely up to parliament: it was merely its existence (and not the Makarrata Commission's) that would be enshrined in the constitution. They reminded the government that there was no veto and no suggestion of establishing a third chamber of parliament; that the Referendum Council had explicitly stated the body would only consider legislation that fell under the "constitutional powers regarding race and territories." They stressed that the council's report had not abandoned symbolic statements of recognition, that it proposed all Australian parliaments pass an "inspiring and unifying" Declaration of Recognition, which reflected Australia's "shared history, heritage and aspirations."

Nor was the advisory body a new idea. In the Kirribilli Statement, issued after their meeting with Abbott and Shorten in July 2015,

Indigenous leaders made clear that the "minimalist" path of symbolic constitutional reform "would not be acceptable" and asked for clarity from both the government and the Opposition on two issues: "prevention of racially discriminatory laws and the proposed advisory body." In 2015, before he became prime minister, Turnbull had privately expressed his support for the idea to Noel Pearson. But as prime minister, in November 2016, he expressed reservations in a meeting with the Referendum Council. Challenged by Pearson to clarify whether he was ruling out the option of an advisory body before the dialogue process even began, Turnbull backtracked, saying he was just "expressing an opinion." One month later, together with Shorten, he wrote to confirm the government's support for the testing of "all models" of constitutional recognition. The dialogues went ahead with the option of an advisory body on the table. But Turnbull had already decided to walk away from it.

None of this is to deny that the proposal for an advisory body had its detractors within the Indigenous political class. Warren Mundine's initial assessment was bleak: "I think you can kiss [the referendum] goodbye," he said. By the time the idea had gained majority support at Uluru in May 2017, the disquiet remained. Mick Dodson, for example, could not hide his disappointment:

> It's not going to deal with the Constitution. The idea that we go cap
> in hand to the parliament and ask them to set up a representative
> body is not dealing with our racist Constitution. Secondly, if we're
> talking about a treaty and having some sort of recognition of at least
> a residuum of Indigenous sovereignty, this concedes our sover-
> eignty upfront. [It suggests we] go to the parliament and say:
> "Please listen to us." … The problem with our policy approach is
> we don't have any power in the game. It's all up there on the hill.

Given that one of the tasks of the proposed Makarrata Commission would be to deal with treaty-making, Dodson may have overstated the "ceding" of sovereignty. The advisory body was one arm of a raft of initiatives. It was not the only one. But his concerns regarding the constitution and the apparent meekness of the advisory body – parliament's supremacy remained absolute – again highlighted the extent of the government's dishonesty in claiming that it would act as a third chamber of parliament.

The Uluru Statement from the Heart was an appeal to the parliament and the people of Australia, one couched in the tradition of the many petitions Indigenous Australians had delivered to the Crown and parliaments of Britain and Australia since the nineteenth century. It was deeply respectful of Australia's parliament and the sovereignty of the crown. It was indeed the cri de coeur: a call for action and unity, and one that will undoubtedly join the Yirrkala bark petitions (1963), the Barunga Statement (1988) and the National Apology to the Stolen Generations (2008) on the walls of Parliament House in Canberra.

Turnbull's failure to "see" the profound historical importance of the Uluru Statement pointed to a far deeper problem: the culture of entrenched "indifference" towards Indigenous Australians, one which W.E.H. Stanner perceptively described in 1977 as "a sightlessness towards Aboriginal life ... and the moral foundation of Australian development." Just as Turnbull had failed to appreciate how the historical experience of Aboriginal people had led to the Uluru Statement, he had also failed to see that his government's contemptuous response was itself an episode in the long history of indifference, discrimination and injustice meted out to Indigenous Australians by colonial, state and federal governments.

It was the parliaments of Australia that had denied Indigenous Australians their rights, taken children from their families and sought to control every aspect of their lives. Whether it was to hasten their extinction or ensure their survival, the meddling hands of governments were all over them. They remain there today. Understand this and you understand the call for an Indigenous advisory body to parliament. Turnbull's brusque dismissal of a proposal that emerged after years of deliberation demonstrated that Australian federal governments are still completely unaccustomed to negotiating with Indigenous peoples as equals.

Consider for a moment the remarkable endurance and patience of Indigenous Australians. Half a century on from the 1967 referendum, they still wait for substantive political and constitutional change to acknowledge their place in the nation. Imagine how it felt to watch as the same-sex marriage campaign (important as it was) and the citizenship imbroglio dominated political debate and pushed to the sidelines the issues you had fought for for so long. For a moment, it seemed that Australians were more preoccupied with the centenary of the Battle of Beersheba – commemorated a mere five days after Turnbull responded to the Referendum Council – than they were with the fate of Indigenous proposals for reform. Would you not feel marginalised? Ignored? Dismissed, yet again? The long campaign to win "a rightful place" for Indigenous Australians in the Commonwealth is one of the most important and pressing issues on our national agenda. It is not a boutique item for political leaders to pick up or drop as the mood takes them. In December 2014, Tony Abbott, the self-appointed "Prime Minister for Indigenous Affairs," promised that he would "sweat blood" to achieve a successful referendum on constitutional recognition. Like so many other prime ministers before and after him, Abbott's intentions were admirable, but his actions in office failed to match his rhetoric. We are no further advanced today.

Where is the sense of urgency? The understanding that this issue is central to the nation's legitimacy, its international standing, its integrity and its dignity? Where is the prime minister who will do what is required and go out, day after day, and make the case for constitutional justice as a matter of national importance? A prime minister who will take a stance and persuade the electorate to support a concrete referendum proposal? Can such a creature be found anymore?

One of the most striking absences from the Turnbull government's press release was the Makarrata Commission. There was no mention of the proposal for a body to oversee treaty-making and truth-telling about the nation's history. The silence was deafening, yet unsurprising. If anything makes a Coalition government uncomfortable, it's facing up to the way the country was conquered. The two most significant acknowledgments by federal governments of historical injustice in the last thirty years – Paul Keating's Redfern Park Speech (1992) and Kevin Rudd's Apology to the Stolen Generations (2008) – have both come from the Labor side of politics. By contrast, John Howard turned the condemnation of "black armband history" into a political calling card for a generation of conservatives.

Yet the reasons for the Turnbull government's disregard go beyond the confines of Liberal political philosophy. As Galarrwuy Yunupingu suggests, they reflect a deeper cultural prejudice. "The Australian people know their success is built on the taking of the land, in making the country their own," he argues, "which they did at the expense of so many languages and ceremonies and songlines – and people – now destroyed. They worry about what has been done for them and on their behalf, and they know that reconciliation requires much more than just words."

Mick Dodson agrees, claiming that there's "something in the Australian psyche that goes back to colonisation and the way in which present-day Australia came by the country and there's fear of facing up to that truth ... we don't want to confront these wrongs and be called to account for them." What Dodson calls "the Australian psyche" Stanner referred to as the "Australian conscience," a state of heart and mind, a moral calculus that was inherently resistant to confronting a profound historical truth: "there was more than an accidental correspondence between the ruin of Aboriginal, and the making of European life in Australia. There was, in fact, a functional concomitance ... the destruction of Aboriginal society was not the consequence of European development, but its price." It's precisely this *recognition* – that the material success of Australian society was built upon the dispossession of Indigenous Australia, a history that clearly demands treaty and settlement – that causes so many to avert their eyes.

In 2017, it was not only the government's response to the Referendum Council that betrayed a deep-seated fear of confronting the past. It was also starkly evident in the public controversy over the inscriptions on colonial statues and the debate over the memorialisation of the frontier wars and the future of Australia Day. Even these disputes are only the surface ripples of a far more prolonged and all-encompassing national project, one that we have yet to see "whole" rather than through its constituent parts – reconciliation and constitutional recognition; the republic; and the recent resurgence of Anzac Day as Australia's national day. All of these designs for national renewal are intimately connected to the challenge of truth-telling and the acknowledgment of history, yet so far we have failed to see the connections between them. We contemplate recognition. We remain divided over the meaning of Australia Day. We gather around the hearth of Anzac. We discuss the republic. But these debates and their histories circulate in parallel universes. This essay is an attempt to bring them together, to yoke a vast body of historical scholarship that has transformed our understanding of Australian history over the past five decades to the deeper currents of a country on the brink of momentous change.

Within the next decade Australia has the opportunity to achieve a meaningful constitutional settlement with Indigenous Australians, to become a republic, and perhaps in the process, to redefine the way we see ourselves and the way the country is seen by others. If these changes are to have any realistic prospect of success, we need to articulate a more cohesive and unified vision, one that understands the crucial importance of truth-telling, together with a fundamental paradox: that acknowledging the past – or, more specifically, what the poet Judith Wright called the "attitudes that helped us to conquer and settle this country" – will not weigh us down. It will liberate us. This applies as much to Indigenous as it does to other Australians.

In his extraordinary essay "Rom Watangu: The Law of the Land," published in the Monthly in July 2016, Galarrwuy Yunupingu recalled how his father, Mungurrawuy, was present "when the massacres occurred in [East Arnhem Land] in the 1920s and 1930s." He was also "shot by a man licensed to do so." "These events and what lies behind them are burned into our minds," he explained. "They are never forgotten. Such things are remembered. Like the scar that marked the exit of the bullet from my father's body." The scars – memories of forced removal, murder, warfare, resistance and survival – are etched into the bloodlines of Australia's historical imagination. In the past, we have dealt with them by repression, silence and denial. But we have yet to understand how we can use them productively. As Marcia Langton wrote in 2003, because of the work of historians and Aboriginal people who have shared their oral histories over the last decades, we now have "a much more robust idea of the past from which Australians need not shrink in denial, but which, if wrestled with honestly, lays the foundations for a new story of the nation." This "new story" is one that we have barely begun to glimpse. Ever so tentatively, we are coming to accept the relationship between the acknowledgment of history and the re-founding of the nation on more honest, just and legitimate grounds.

The cultures and histories of Indigenous Australia that were believed to be destined for extinction at the time of Federation in 1901 have not merely resurfaced, they have moved from the periphery of Australia's national imagination to its centre, where they rightly belong. This gradual transformation – the rise of the very presence that had allegedly been vanquished – represents the most significant shift in Australia's historical consciousness since European settlement began. And its expression is central to the new constitutional settlement we are striving to accomplish. Many writers before me – historians, novelists, lawyers, artists, journalists, theologians, politicians, anthropologists, political scientists and countless more – have grappled with the complex relationship between history, constitutional justice and national legitimacy. This is a collaborative project. And we have to take the long view.

Since the 1970s, Australia has been struggling with the challenge of founding what Noel Pearson has eloquently called a "more complete Commonwealth." No longer able to rely on the old narratives that sustained what was seen as an isolated, essentially British society in the South Pacific, and confronting a rising tide of Indigenous protest and revisionist history which exposed the lie of peaceful British settlement, the country has witnessed an ongoing crisis of faith in its legitimacy. At the heart of this crisis is a dispute about the way the country was conquered and settled – the long history of Australia's frontier. The very first Quarterly Essay, Robert Manne's *In Denial: The Stolen Generations and the Right* (2001), interpreted the bitter debate over the release of the Australian Human Rights Commission's *Bringing Them Home* report (1997) as a symptom of a much longer-lasting and "larger culture war – over the meaning of Aboriginal dispossession."

Sixteen years later, we are still trying to understand the *meaning* of this history and its significance for the nation's future. The question of whether Australia Day should be moved – debated in one form or another since the commemoration of Governor Arthur Phillip's arrival at Sydney Cove began in earnest in the nineteenth century – is merely the latest example. But it is also a sign of a slowly dawning realisation: the way we acknowledge our history has the power to make or unmake the nation. If we really intend to found a more complete Commonwealth, are we prepared to change the way we represent the nation's past and include the perspective of Indigenous Australians? Are we willing to honour the democratic process and Indigenous consensus that underwrites the Uluru Statement? And can we find the political will to transcend the bitter divisions that have plagued public discussion of the country's history for so long? A bird's-eye view of Australia's culture in 2018 suggests that we remain deeply divided over the way the country was founded.

Our government dismisses the Uluru Statement from the Heart, refusing to embrace a truth-telling commission. Our legal and political system grapples with questions of native title and the ongoing legacies of the frontier in remote communities. Our schools, universities and media debate the terminology we should use to describe the arrival of the First Fleet in 1788 and how much emphasis we should place on invasion and dispossession, while on Australia Day this year tens of thousands cried "change the date," as they marched in cities and towns around the country. Our journalists, historians, poets, playwrights, novelists, artists, composers, scriptwriters, filmmakers, dancers and curators produce work that deals with the troubling inheritance of the frontier. Our citizens erect memorials to those killed in massacres and violent encounters. Our clergy and community leaders speak of the need for reconciliation and recognition. More than any other history, the history of the frontier continues to unsettle and trouble us – we rake over the embers, endlessly searching for redemption.

27 October 2017: the day after the Turnbull government's rejection of the Referendum Council's final report. The room at the Australian National University in Canberra was full of historians and students who had come to celebrate the fortieth anniversary of the founding of *Aboriginal History*, the journal that signalled a new focus on "the post-contact history of the Aborigines and Torres Strait Islanders."

Bain Attwood, one of Australia's leading scholars of colonialism, reminded the audience of the mission of the journal's founders. They wanted to place Aboriginal people at the centre of their research rather than "in the footnotes." Drawing on oral traditions and ethnographic knowledge, they would seek out authors who could highlight Aboriginal voices and offer an Aboriginal perspective on the past; Aboriginal people would be seen as agents of change rather than mere victims of imperialism. They saw the new field as comparative, predominantly local and regional in focus, dispassionate and apolitical. They would publish histories that went beyond resistance, frontier violence and cultural annihilation, and instead uncovered the full range of the cross-cultural encounter: astonishment, curiosity, bewilderment, the sharing of knowledge, cohabitation and interdependence, accommodation, adaptation and cultural survival. Warfare and conflict over land were not the sum total of Australia's creation.

Forty years later, it's striking how many of these concerns remain priorities for historians. Yet it's also impossible not to notice the gulf between academic historians' perceptions of their work and popular understandings of the history of contact between Indigenous people and British settlers. While historians have long sought to write deeply researched, fine-grained, empathetic and nuanced histories that cover the gamut of human experience, public perceptions of Australia's frontiers often focus on violence and its consequences. Our failure to resolve debates over the future of Australia Day, colonial statues and the much larger challenge of establishing a national truth-telling commission only tends to push public discussion of Australian history into a familiar succession of conflicting binaries. I've lost count of the times during radio interviews that I've been asked to explain whether Australia was invaded or settled. And I often feel that the line of questioning – the demand for a verdict, followed by conviction (or acquittal); a past that can fit neatly onto a flag and be waved from on high – runs counter to everything I've worked for as a historian.

One question that was asked that day in Canberra took everyone aback. The filmmaker and historian Frances Peters-Little threw it as friendly bait to the audience. "One thing that I've always wanted to know," she said, "is why you whitefellas are interested in blackfella history." It's a question that has stayed with me. At the time, I said that I found it impossible to live in this country as an informed citizen without understanding Aboriginal history and culture. But the question kept nagging at me, and I left knowing I hadn't answered it adequately. Frances had forced me to go back to the beginning.

The starting point was undoubtedly 1977. As a first-year arts student at the University of Sydney, majoring in English literature and European and American history, I was asked to write an essay for my anthropology course on Stanner's acclaimed 1968 ABC Boyer Lectures, *After the Dreaming*. My high-school education had taught me much about the reasons for the collapse of the Weimar Republic and the rise of Nazism – even if their histories were reduced to "key events and arguments" for frenzied regurgitation in a 45-minute essay – but I realised I had next to no knowledge of the history of my own country.

As I struggled, like so many first-year students, with the convoluted and detached nature of much academic prose – "as the present author contends" – Stanner's lectures came as a relief. The writing moved me intellectually and emotionally. The voice was fearless, lyrical and incisive. Stanner possessed a scholarly clarity and moral conviction I'd encountered in no other writer handed to me on a university reading list. I suddenly realised that I was entirely ignorant of the central drama of Australian history: the encounter between Aboriginal people and the strangers who came across the seas to claim their lands. Stanner's unforgettable metaphor, "the Great Australian Silence" – among the most quoted phrases in Australian historical writing – described a "cult of forgetfulness practised on a national scale." Yet it wasn't only this idea that stayed with me, but his underlying tone: a contempt for white indifference coupled with a quality I had rarely if ever encountered growing up in Sydney in the 1960s and 1970s: a respect and awe for Aboriginal culture and the fundamental humanity of Aboriginal people.

At the time, I had no intention of becoming a historian. Although the personal resonance of Stanner's lectures was undeniable and enduring, the urge to research and write Australian history unfolded gradually. Living in Germany as a somewhat exotic specimen in the 1980s and fielding questions about Australia, I remember often being asked: "What about the Indigenous people?" It seemed that my German friends were more interested in this question than my friends at home. Again, I was forced to acknowledge my ignorance. I returned to Australia convinced that I needed to know more about Australian history. Yet even then, after I enrolled in an MA under Donald Horne at the University of New South Wales, my initial research interest was not Aboriginal history, but the history of republicanism in Australia. With Paul Keating leading the push in the early 1990s – the first and only Australian prime minister to shape the long-held dream of a republic into a concrete proposal for constitutional reform – it was an exciting time to be working on the history of the republican ideal. My historical research fed into a receptive political environment. It was relevant in a way few other topics could have been. For several years, I made my daily pilgrimage to the State Library of New South Wales – Queen Elizabeth II and Prince Philip waving to me encouragingly from their Daimler as they drove along Macquarie Street in 1992 – hoping to unearth a history that might inform the kind of republic we were about to become.

If there was a turning point in my slow awakening to Indigenous Australia, it came in 1993, when I purchased ten acres of land on the far south coast of New South Wales. More than any work of history or literature I had read, it was my physical presence on a patch of relatively "unsettled" country that transformed my understanding. Questions that had previously appeared academic suddenly became deeply personal. What was the history of the property (a word that quickly seemed inappropriate) before the fences? Before it was surveyed, mapped, named, carved into allotments and sold? Before the riverbed filled with tonnes of sediment from road-building and land-clearing? Before the homesteads dug in and the telegraph lines marched across the land? Could thousands of years of human habitation be obliterated in a mere 150 years of settler occupation? What had happened in the wake of the settler invasion? Was it even possible to understand how the country was perceived by Aboriginal people, to grasp something of its inherent Aboriginality? For the first time, history became tangible in a way it had never seemed to be before. If there was a moment when the direction of my work changed irrevocably, this was it.

The questions became the starting point of a book – *Looking for Blackfellas' Point* – published in 2002, in which I tried to connect the story of my presence on the land to the history of southeastern New South Wales and the larger controversies (or "wars") concerning Australian history that were dominating public debate at the time, particularly the question of an apology to the Stolen Generations and the bitter debate over the number of Aboriginal people killed on the frontier that was sparked by the 2001 publication of Keith Windschuttle's *The Fabrication of Aboriginal History*. In the process of writing the book, I came to understand how the invaders and their descendants had fostered a "culture of forgetting" regarding Aboriginal people and their violent dispossession. In the history of one region, I found much of the nation's history writ large. What had previously been generic debates about frontier violence or the Stolen Generations were now lit brightly in the everyday lives of people in local communities. In town halls, clubs and schools, people listened as Aboriginal men and women told their stories of being removed from their families and explained how every waking moment of their lives had been micromanaged by the state. For Aboriginal people on the far south coast, history was not past. Nor was it a heritage item to be renovated and frozen in time for the tourist industry. It was lived every day. Not so much a series of events as a tidal force that altered their lives forever. As Galarrwuy Yunupingu later described his people's experience in East Arnhem Land, "it was a wave of history that broke over us, and that we had to contend with."

After writing Looking for Blackfellas' Point, I returned to my earlier work on the republic and saw the glaring blind spot in my thinking. Like much of the contemporary republican movement, I had assumed that the whole question of a republic could be advanced through the traditional Anglo-Australian axis – breaking away from Britain and becoming fully independent with our own head of state – with little reference to Indigenous Australia. I had failed to see the connection that now seems so obvious: if we remove the sovereignty of the Crown and reconstitute the Commonwealth as a republic, then we must acknowledge "the first sovereign nations of the continent and its adjacent islands." How could we imagine reconstituting the sovereignty of the Australian people as a republic, while ignoring Indigenous Australians yet again? To work through these questions, I wrote a small book – This Country: A Reconciled Republic? (2004) – which argued that the two movements for national renewal that had previously travelled on parallel lines, largely without addressing one another, needed to think harder about the connections between them. Fourteen years later, with both questions still unresolved, these connections seem even more obvious.

Whatever form they finally take, recognition and reconciliation must take place before the republic. To do otherwise, regardless of when the Queen dies, would be to suggest that the position of Indigenous Australians in our constitution and national life is secondary to severing ties with the Crown. We should not contemplate such an insult. Recognition and the republic are, in fact, two giant and interrelated steps we must take if we are to re-found the Commonwealth on a more just and democratic basis. Both are part of the legacy of colonialism. Both challenge us to re-found the Commonwealth in a way that reflects the aspirations of Australia in the early twenty-first century. The only republic worth having is a reconciled republic. As the Uluru Statement from the

Heart explained, Indigenous sovereignty is a "spiritual notion" – the "ancestral tie" between Aboriginal people and the land – that "has never been ceded or extinguished." While it implicitly "coexists with the sovereignty of the Crown" today, it must explicitly coexist with the sovereignty of the Australian people in a future republican constitution. In other words, an Australian republic must make visible what the Crown for so long denied. Republicans have to talk about more than the head of state alone. After all, it is not the head of state who will be sovereign in our future republic, but the people themselves. For this reason alone, republicans need to provide a more convincing rationale for change, one that is grounded in the "spiritual" sovereignty of Indigenous Australia and the country itself, not merely in removal of the monarchy. Indigenous recognition and truth-telling are integral to that vision. Realising this is another way of saying that Aboriginal history, politics and culture cannot be cordoned off from any part of Australian life. "Their" history can never be separated from "our" history. After 1788, our cultures and histories became permanently entangled, each altered irrevocably by the other. We were bound together. And we cannot write one history without the other.

If this explains "how" I came to be interested in "blackfella history" – without mentioning the influence of the work of friends and colleagues who undertook similar journeys and who have published far more widely on Aboriginal history than I have – it only partly explains the "why." Every writer and reader of Australian history will have their own answer. From my own experience, I can only say that knowledge of blackfella history has become integral to my sense of being Australian. It is no longer a choice that I consciously make. When we speak of a culture of forgetting in Australia, it is not just the frontier and dispossession that the nation has been busily forgetting. It is the forgetting of a whole culture, a whole way of seeing the land. Aboriginal people had a name for every plant, creature and landform in the continent. Much of the detail of that cultural knowledge, embedded in ceremony, songlines and every aspect of their daily lives, has been lost forever in many parts of the country. Walking along the river that runs through my land on the far south coast, I know that Aboriginal people walked the same riverbed, camped on its banks and flats, and saw the country in a way I will never be able to entirely grasp or understand.

Because our understanding of the depth and complexity of Indigenous cultures is expanding constantly, every new revelation, every new piece of research and writing – whether it be history, fiction, art, theatre, dance or song – holds out the promise of seeing this country differently. One word from an Indigenous language can transform our understanding. The Burrup Peninsula in the Pilbara – named by Woodside Petroleum in 1979 – was known by its custodians, the Yaburara, as "Murujuga" – "hip bone sticking out" – an image that embodies the protruding contours of the peninsula as no whitefella name could. Every time I drive the Snowy Mountains Highway south of Cooma and look out across the bare grassy hills of the Monaro plains, I remember that John Lhotsky, the Polish naturalist who explored the Monaro in early 1834 and transcribed one of the first specimens of Australian music – "Song of the Women of the Menero Tribe" – also recorded that the Aboriginal word monaro translated into English as "like a woman's breast," an image that perfectly evokes the curved lines of the bare, rounded hills that rise on the Monaro plains. Merging body and earth, it opens up another way of perceiving the land, a "spiritual sovereignty" that can only be comprehended by listening to and learning from Indigenous Australians, although it can never be fully known by anyone other than its true custodians.

Wrestling with silence – Stanner's Great Australian Silence – continues to draw me back to blackfella history. No part of Australia was left untouched by frontier violence. The humanity of Indigenous Australians was denied by governments and local authorities in every state and territory. Aboriginal people have never been compensated for the loss of their lands. Given their relative invisibility in the constitution, they remain outsiders in their own country. As one of more than 24 million current beneficiaries of their dispossession and cultural richness, I don't believe it is possible to understand the country I live in today without understanding how the country was taken from them. The legacy of that history is alive in every aspect of our culture and politics, and remains unresolved.

One of the most remarkable things about Stanner's metaphor is its durability. Henry Reynolds pronounced the death of the Great Australian Silence as long ago as 1984, when he argued that the amount of work on "Aboriginal history" had already shattered the pervasive culture of silence that descended on Australia in the twentieth century regarding the dispossession of Indigenous Australians. Despite the enormous body of scholarship published since that time, we frequently revert to Stanner's metaphor – in 2013, Prime Minister Julia Gillard described the absence of Indigenous recognition in the Australian constitution as "the Great Australian Silence" – even if only to measure the slow progress Australia has made in confronting its past. Yet today we find ourselves in a radically different situation.

When Stanner delivered his Boyer Lectures in 1968, Australia remained a culturally homogenous society. The Australian Bureau of Statistics broke the country's population of just under 12 million into three broad categories: "British: Born in Australia" (9.5 million), "British: Born Overseas" (1.6 million) and "Foreign" (500,000). As if to make Stanner's point, the opening chapter of the Bureau's 1968 Year Book – "Discovery, Colonisation, and Federation of Australia" – made no mention of Indigenous Australians, while its tally of the Aboriginal population (80,000) counted only "persons of 50 per cent or more Aboriginal blood." Stanner's audience – his "we" – was the overwhelming "British" majority. It was Australian Britons and their ancestors who had created the "Great Australian Silence."

Almost fifty years later, the 2016 Census revealed that just over 28 per cent of the nation's population of 24 million were born overseas, with more than a third of their number coming from Asia. Casting his eye over this new demographic landscape, George Megalogenis points out that "just under half the [country's] total population [today] is either first or second generation Australian." Despite its uneven geographical spread, this migration boom – the most profound, Megalogenis argues, "since the gold rushes of the 1850s" – has cemented Australia's "Eurasian" future.

Where does this leave the future history of European Australia? If we take the long view, like renowned archaeologist Mike Smith, it will be seen as a brief but significant moment in time, wedged between the deep past of Aboriginal Australia and the deep future of Asian Australia.

Exactly how debates about the legacy of British colonisation and the dispossession of Indigenous Australians speak to the large proportion of recently arrived migrants is difficult to tell. What stake do they feel they have in these discussions? Do they feel implicated? Or do they feel they are watching as if from the outside? No doubt there are myriad different responses, as there would be for any demographic group in Australia. But given the radically altered composition of Australian society today, its extraordinary cultural diversity, its restless, forward-looking disposition, and the surfeit of historical knowledge that has become available to an increasingly educated society over the last fifty years, it's no longer tenable to talk in the way that Stanner did about a "cult of forgetfulness" practised on a "national scale." That time is past. The burgeoning campaign to change the date of Australia Day is one indication of this change. A new fount of historical knowledge has altered our view of the past and the way we seek to represent the nation in the future. The centre of gravity has slowly shifted towards a more complex, yet ultimately richer and more honest history that continues to unsettle us. If recent Australian art, film and literature is any barometer, the country remains haunted by the violence and dispossession at the nation's foundation.

Peter Carey, whose latest novel, *A Long Way from Home* (2017), tells the story of a couple from Western Victoria in the 1950s who take part in the Redex Trial, a cross-country Australian car race, and stumble upon massacre sites where hundreds of Indigenous people died, admitted recently that he would feel "shameful," if, in a "life of writing," he failed to address the "landscape of colonialism in Australia." The towns and pastoral properties that Carey's characters pass through on their journey, all marked prominently on the map, soon give way to the ancient maps of Indigenous songlines.

Kim Scott's novel *Taboo*, published only three months before Carey's, also deals with the legacy of frontier violence, and one massacre in particular, which took place in the early 1880s at Cocanarup, near Ravensthorpe, in Scott's Noongar homeland. An article that appeared in a West Australian newspaper in 1935 unremorsefully described how "members on the station were then granted license to shoot the natives [around Ravensthorpe] for a period of one month, during which time the fullest advantage was taken of the privilege." For Scott's family and clan (the Wirlomin), the site of the massacre has long been "taboo." Forced to live with the horrific memories of what was done to their ancestors (like so many Aboriginal people throughout Australia), they have been unable to bring themselves to visit the "killing place." Meanwhile, the novel's non-Indigenous characters struggle to accept what happened and deny any suggestion of a "massacre." As Scott tells the story of recent attempts to reconcile the history through the establishment of a "Peace Park" and the erection of a memorial, taboos abound on both sides.

Scott's and Carey's novels are only two recent examples of "reconciliation literature," and it would be possible to choose any number from the past few decades, including Kate Grenville's *The Secret River* (2005) and Alex Miller's *Landscape of Farewell* (2007). Fiction aside, a wave of recent productions have drawn on histories of frontier violence, including Warwick Thornton's latest film, *Sweet Country* (2018), which tells the story of an Aboriginal station-hand in the 1920s who murders a station owner in self-defence, and takes flight with his wife in the MacDonnell Ranges. In 2016, *The Names of Places*, an interactive multimedia work created by Waanyi artist Judy Watson, showed massacre sites across the country and invited members of the audience with their own massacre stories to contribute to a constantly expanding database and website. In 2017, the Melbourne Museum launched a new exhibit, *Black Day, Sun Rises, Blood Runs*, which includes film of Indigenous people across Victoria telling their massacre stories in the places where the events took place. In 2014, Paul Stanhope's composition for choir and symphony orchestra, *Jandamarra – Sing for the Country*, performed at the Sydney Opera House, told the story of a Bunuba warrior from the Kimberley in the late nineteenth century. Jandamarra was both an outcast because of his work as a police tracker and a hero because of his last-minute decision to turn against the colonial authorities in order to save his own people. When police finally killed him in 1897, they cut off his head as a trophy of their victory and shipped it to England, where it remains today.

In their different ways, all these works of art confront the legacies of colonialism, all grapple with violence and dispossession, and all point in one way or other to the need for healing and reconciliation. Yet the question remains: exactly how much of the knowledge from the new Aboriginal history has seeped through into wider society? The historian Tom Griffiths recently described "the endemic forgetfulness of the dominant culture" in Australia, as if to suggest that little of the new history has permeated broader public consciousness, or that even when it does, the knowledge does not stick. Australians seem to be always in need of re-education. Our embrace of the past is conveniently selective. We go to extraordinary lengths to keep the flame of Anzac alive at the same time as we reduce the history of our frontier to a mere "blemish" in the story of the nation's success. Over the last half-century, our political leaders have lurched from humble recognition of dispossession to shameless evasion.

In 1992, in his Redfern Park speech, Prime Minister Paul Keating said, "It was we who did the dispossessing. We took the traditional lands and smashed the traditional way of life. We brought the diseases. The alcohol. We committed the murders. We took the children from their mothers. We practised discrimination and exclusion. It was our ignorance and our prejudice."

In 2003, Prime Minister John Howard told a gathering at the Supreme Court of Victoria that Australia had "formed a nation without strife or warfare," as if the frontier wars were a figment of historians' imaginations. Denial of the country's violent foundation has continued to coexist with acknowledgment.

The truth is that the history wars of recent decades have left us with competing narratives of the nation's foundation. The silence may have lifted, but the state's failure to acknowledge fully the historical experience of Indigenous Australians in the wake of British colonisation remains.

In 2012, the booklet that the Australian government distributed to new citizens (*Australian Citizenship: Our Common Bond*) included a "testable section" of civic knowledge. It opened with a short passage on "Australia and its people," which jumped from "Indigenous Australians" to the "Early Days of European Settlement" to the "Nation of Australia" without mentioning frontier conflict or the exclusion of Indigenous Australians. "Practice test questions" for this section predictably asked: "What do we remember on Anzac Day?"

When the impact of disease, frontier conflict and loss of Indigenous lives was finally acknowledged in the brief historical overview offered in the booklet's "non-testable section," some of the language would have made John Howard proud: "Apart from small-scale battles between settlers and the Aboriginal people, Australia has been a remarkably peaceful country. There have been no civil wars or revolutions." "Small-scale"? Compared to Passchendaele or the Battle of Stalingrad, the battles on the Australian frontier were indeed "small-scale." But when we consider that there were countless battles across the entire continent over a period of nearly 150 years, in which tens of thousands of Aboriginal people and thousands of settlers died, it is clear that they were of profound significance for the nation's foundation. Predictably, the citizenship booklet moved on swiftly, devoting two pages to World War I and the Anzac Legend. In the latest edition of the same booklet, "small-scale battles" has been replaced by a more generic term, "conflict." Yet the emphasis remains on Australia's "peaceful history," a lie of immeasurable proportions.

In the nineteenth and early twentieth centuries, "warfare" and "invasion" were terms frequently used to describe the nature of frontier conflict in Australia. These words are not the latter-day invention of left-leaning historians. If we have difficulty in admitting the existence of frontier wars to our new citizens, what hope is there that the nation will embrace truth-telling on a national scale? It seems that we have yet to grasp the lessons that can be learnt from *Aboriginal History*.

LISTENING TO INDIGENOUS VOICES

It was the first time in Australia's history that such an extensive process of consultation had taken place. Beginning in 2016 and culminating at Uluru in May 2017, the Referendum Council conducted twelve dialogues with more than a thousand people in Indigenous communities across Australia. A common refrain in all of these discussions, although it barely featured in media coverage, was the demand for truth-telling. One "truth" above all others was referred to repeatedly: "What happened all across Australia: the massacres and the wars." More than any other aspect of Australian history since the British arrived in 1788, it was this truth that Indigenous Australians wanted told.

It was a demand that had long been frustrated by the failure of governments to keep their word. In the winter of 1988, Prime Minister Bob Hawke promised a treaty with Indigenous Australians, by which time, he assured them, "a position will have been reached in which the non-Aboriginal people will recognise the injustices of the past." Neither the treaty nor Hawke's recognition of past injustice came to pass. Perhaps it was not surprising, given that six months earlier, when he delivered his Australia Day address in the Sydney Opera House forecourt to a nation-wide TV audience, Hawke made no mention of Indigenous Australians. By the time Kevin Rudd delivered the National Apology to the Stolen Generations in February 2008, after more than a decade's resistance from the Howard government, it may have felt like a "nationwide emotional release" and a "gesture of atonement for the full disastrous history of indigenous relations since 1988," as the *Sydney Morning Herald*'s editorial pleaded, but Rudd had not addressed the frontier wars. This is the line the nation still struggles to cross. When we begin public meetings and official events with an acknowledgment of country, we refer to Aboriginal people as "traditional owners of the land," a phrase that lacks a completing clause: "which was taken from them without their consent, treaty or compensation." Even our acknowledgments contain silences.

Australians knew of the existence of the American frontier before they had any conception of a frontier on their own continent. Growing up in the 1970s, and watching endless re-runs of American westerns on TV, I knew the names of Indian chiefs – Sitting Bull, Cochise and Geronimo – long before I had heard of Pemulwuy, Yagan or Windradyne. I knew the Apache, the Sioux and the Cherokee before I knew of the Eora, Noongar and Wiradjuri. It often seemed that American cultural references were more familiar than the people and places of my own country. While frontier expansion was firmly embedded in America's national imagination, thanks largely to the impact of Frederick Jackson Turner's seminal essay, "The Significance of the Frontier in American History" (1893), which cultivated the legend of settlers taking up "free land" and "winning a wilderness," Australia's frontier experience was largely banished from the national consciousness, even though it was here, on the plains, hills and river banks of this country, that Australia was created.

Between 1788 and the outbreak of World War I, more than 22 million British emigrants left their homes to settle in North America, Australia, New Zealand and southern Africa. The history of Australia's frontier is one part of this global story of British imperial expansion. It is also exceptional in at least one crucial respect: Australia was unique among British colonies in being colonised without treaty. In stark contrast to other British colonies, the continent was conquered without negotiation with its Indigenous people. As Henry Reynolds explained, "the whole venture was premised on the belief . . . that the Aborigines had no legitimate claim on the land." This not only meant that the land was taken without compensation, but, as Bain Attwood has shown recently, it left following generations without a redeeming narrative – unlike Canada or New Zealand, Australia has no treaty story to fall back on when explaining how settlers took possession of the land. Our turning away from the history of the frontier and silencing of the true history of the country's foundation was in many ways an entirely understandable response. Aside from a thin strand of humanitarian concern, much of it expressed far from the front line of contact, there was no honourable peg on which to hang the story of conquest.

In the years since a pioneering generation of historians "opened up" the history of the frontier in the 1970s and 1980s, a flood of new scholarship – history, archaeology, anthropology, geology, linguistics, scientific research employing new technologies and a deep well of Indigenous oral history – has transformed our understanding of Aboriginal cultures and the way in which the continent was claimed and conquered by Europeans. Many longstanding beliefs have been shattered. Archaeological research has confirmed what Indigenous Australians already knew: they have occupied the continent for at least 65,000 years. Weighed against the depth of Indigenous antiquity, the words proposed to recognise Indigenous Australians in the constitution ("original custodians") appear lame and inadequate. Equally, when we tell our new citizens that "Aboriginal people did not grow crops or set up homes to stay in one place as the British did," we are peddling falsehoods. British settlers arrived to a carefully managed landscape. It was not natural. There was no wilderness or "empty places." Aboriginal people built villages, cultivated and harvested crops, dried and stored food, constructed elaborate stone walls, quarries, fish traps, terraced gardens, paths and fences. Australian "civilisation" was already established. The challenge of incorporating Indigenous ecological knowledge – firestick farming is perhaps the most obvious example – into the way we care for country today is one that we have only recently taken up. As the Yuin elder Ossie Cruse insists, the task of reconciliation is two-fold: to establish "equitable sovereignty" and to ensure that all Australians, drawing on Indigenous knowledge, share "equal custodianship" of the land and environment.

The frontier that followed in the wake of the British invasion was not the first in Australia's history. Aboriginal people in the north of the continent had been trading with Makassan fishermen, who had visited seasonally since at least the eighteenth century, if not before. They learnt to speak Makassan. They travelled with them to present-day Indonesia and beyond. They traded with them, fought with them and made love with them. Relations varied from place to place. Apart from occasional visits by Dutch, French and possibly Portuguese explorers, Aboriginal people encountered the British as the first invaders of their lands. From the outset, the frontier this invasion set in train was never neatly divided between two sides, so much as a murky, entangled terrain which encompassed every possible human interaction. Its geographical reach was as vast as its temporal spread. The continent was not possessed and conquered in one moment in time, but in piecemeal fashion. The speed and influx of settlers, who were often fearful and eager for governments to protect them from Aboriginal attacks, varied from one region to the next. Governments failed to police the frontier effectively. They gave lip service to protecting the rights of "the natives," while aiding and abetting the settlers' dispossession of Aboriginal people. On this note, one of the most damning indictments I have read came from the pen of Catholic archbishop John Bede Polding, who wrote candidly to his superiors in the Vatican in 1846, reflecting on the state of the Aborigines in New South Wales:

> the Portuguese and Spanish in the Americas hunted the poor natives like beasts and obliged them to work in the mines like slaves ... The settlers in Australia seem determined to imitate their conquering predecessors! It is true that the government promises to protect the Aborigines and passes laws and bans in their defence, but then does nothing to apply them. The government spends large amounts to civilise them but, most of the time, the money ends up in the hands of people with large families who call themselves the Protectors of the Aborigines ... In order to comprehend the situation better, these poor people, who have lost their native land to the invaders who destroy and scatter their crops and animals, sometimes, especially in winter, driven by hunger, attempt to retaliate against the Europeans. This results in bloody conflicts which the negroes always lose and this is the source of their hatred towards the whites and consequent

reticence in embracing religion. A short time before I left Sydney, the government called a meeting that they call the "Select Committee on the condition of the Aborigines" ... I was also invited to inform and advise; I was happy to plead in favour of their cause and to suggest ways to prevent their total extermination. God knows what use will be made of my charitable suggestions by the people deciding the fate of the poor Negroes! And, indeed, considering the questions they asked me, I'm afraid that the sole aim of all these conferences is to get the most advantage out of the work of those poor wretches!

Polding was in the process of setting up the first Catholic missions in Australia, which he believed would save the Aborigines from the brutality of the British settlers, and by converting them to Christianity "dissipate the darkness of their natural ignorance." But his reflections on the injustice and violence perpetrated by "the invaders" at a time when New South Wales was beginning to entertain self-government, demonstrates yet again that the prosperity of colonial Australia and the nation that emerged in 1901 was "born" not on the dunes of Anzac Cove, but on the Cumberland Plain, the pastures of Port Phillip and the banks of the Derwent. The establishment of Australia's democratic institutions and its economic development are intimately connected with the "bloody conflicts" over land that Polding condemned. Colonial expansion assumed the death of traditional Indigenous societies. Their only chance of survival was to avoid the invaders as best they could, or shed their culture and live like their usurpers.

Henry Reynolds, the historian who over the past forty years has probably done more than any other writer to haul the history of the frontier into public consciousness, has described settler–Indigenous violence as "one of the most persistent features of Australian life for 140 years." This violence was not entirely inevitable. It was also a path that was chosen consciously by governments and settlers. From 1790, when Governor Arthur Phillip ordered Watkin Tench and a party of over fifty to arrest two "natives" and to put to death six in reprisal for the killing of his gamekeeper by Pemulwuy, punitive expeditions were deployed to demonstrate the invaders' superior power.

"We were to cut off, and bring in the heads of the slain," reported Tench. Marching with great difficulty through the heath and marshlands that once covered the site close to where Sydney airport now stands, Tench and his men carried hatchets to decapitate their victims and large bags for carrying the heads of six Aboriginal men to Sydney Cove. Unable to find his prey and exasperated by the country through which he was moving – "a rotten spungy bog into which we were plunged knee-deep at every step" – he eventually returned to Sydney Cove empty-handed. In 1802, after leading many successful raids on government farms to the west of Sydney, Pemulwuy was killed, and his head was cut off and placed in spirits by Governor Philip Gidley King before being shipped to England. In the years ahead, Phillip's strategy of using violence to teach Aboriginal people "a lesson" would be repeated countless times across the continent.

In 1928, Gallipoli veteran and ace marksman Mounted Constable William George Murray led a punitive expedition that killed scores of Aboriginal people in Central Australia. What became known as the Coniston Massacre was Australia's last officially recorded massacre. But similar expeditions were still being planned in the 1930s. Few Australians realise that at the same moment Don Bradman was leading Australia's defence against England's bodyline bowling in 1932, the residents of Darwin were "seething with indignation" after several murders in north-east Arnhem Land, and demanding that "the natives" at Caledon Bay be "taught a lesson." The planned punitive expedition was only called off at the last minute by the Lyons government due to mounting national and international pressure. The Australian frontier is not a distant phenomenon residing in the dim colonial past. The "killing times" are also part of the history of modern Australia, and they burn in the memories of both Aboriginal and non-Aboriginal Australians.

Historians such as Reynolds, Lyndall Ryan and Ray Evans have provided overwhelming evidence of the role both state-sanctioned and privately conducted violence played in Australia's foundation. Again, it's not uncommon to encounter people reacting with surprise or disbelief when they're confronted with the extent of massacres across the continent. Why has it taken so long for this aspect of our history to imprint itself on the national imagination?

The answers lie in much of the new scholarship on Aboriginal history. Lyndall Ryan's ongoing project to create an interactive online map of massacre sites across Australia – places where six or more people were killed in frontier conflict between 1788 and 1960 – has already attracted widespread national and international attention. The first stage, mapping over 150 massacre sites in eastern Australia, was released in June 2017. Ryan, who has since been flooded with emails and enquiries, has been overwhelmed and heartened by the response, especially from regional Australia, where she believes there is an even stronger desire to know the truth than in urban areas, perhaps because massacre stories tap directly into the family histories of many Aboriginal and non-Aboriginal families still living close to where the events allegedly took place.

While the question of genocide on the frontier has certainly pushed historians to scrutinise the intentions of colonial governments, Ryan feels the term "massacre" is received by people who see her map with more openness than "genocide," which, in her experience, "only makes peoples' eyes glaze over" because it conjures images of the Holocaust and is perceived as a final judgment that ends conversation. Ryan has also been transparent in her presentation of evidence. "The biggest argument in the scholarship of massacre," she explains, is "how do we know it happened? Most massacres took place in secret and were designed not to be discovered, so finding evidence of them is a major challenge. With this map, we've developed a template to identify massacres and a process to corroborate disparate sources ... settler diaries, newspaper reports, Aboriginal evidence and archives from state and federal repositories." By the time the map is completed in 2019, she believes that her research team will have verified more than 500 massacre sites nationwide.

Because so much historical scholarship on the frontier has been local or regional in focus – although Henry Reynolds' recent book *The Forgotten War* summarised much of the national picture, we still await a nationwide history – Australians have yet to truly "see" the imprint of violence in their history on a national scale. This is one reason why Lyndall Ryan's map is having such an impact. Scanning the entire continent, we see hundreds of massacre sites at a glance. The scale of the violence is immediately apparent. No "quadrant of the landscape" is obscured. The sites glow individually as precise geographical coordinates, yet cumulatively they become something much more: a cartographic memorial, a shimmering testimony to a moral truth which is at once overwhelming and undeniable. Though "unbuilt," they stand in our mind's eye with the countless war memorials already scattered across the Australian landscape. Their history suddenly becomes tangible, all-encompassing and potentially nation-defining.

For the Indigenous participants in the Referendum Council dialogues, there was another way in which the history of massacres was silenced in Australia. As they explained, they felt that their voices had not been heard. They had heard historians speak. Now they wanted to tell the story and they wanted Australia to listen. This is why they called for a truth-telling commission. They wanted an opportunity to tell their stories of massacre and injustice, inherited or experienced. These are not all stories of victimhood. Many are stories of heroic resistance and survival. There are now Indigenous oral histories which, building on an already formidable archive collected since the 1960s, document this in harrowing and heartbreaking detail. I could quote examples from every state and territory – accounts of mass shootings and rape, the burning of bodies, and countless stories of indiscriminate terror and violence. Much of this recent oral history emanates from the north of the continent, where many Aboriginal people today have firsthand experience of frontier violence and remember it vividly. The sample below includes eyewitness testimony of individual murders and torture, accounts of massacres and general statements regarding the theft of Aboriginal land. The voices are typical of those the Referendum Council wants Australians to hear in a Truth and Reconciliation Commission.

Those Kartiya (whitefellas) were rotten to the core. I saw them do these things with my own eyes when I was a child ... After Reid [the station manager] shot my great-uncle [Jangari], he got his body and told them, "Take this down there on the plain." Then he dumped wood over my great-uncle. I was bawling by then. My mother was crying for him too, absolutely sobbing. And I was racing around, crying like a mad thing. I was absolutely stunned when I saw my great-uncle get shot. Yeah, I was in total shock. I'd never seen anything like it before. I was in that much grief when the kartiya shot him, put him on a wagonette and carried him off on it. I watched as the kartiya took him to a big plain. They threw wood over him and set his body alight and burnt him right there. The early kartiya did this sort of thing all the time. They used to tie ngumpit [blackfellas] up too, even the policemen did. I witnessed all of this as a kid. They didn't take the side of the ngumpit or stop the kartiya from doing this.

Jimmy Manngayarri

Another crime I witnessed was what they did to Jack Pingkiyarri ... this was before Wave Hill Station moved from the original site on the Victoria River to Jinparrak ... That's the time I saw Jack Pingkiyarri being beaten. He ran away from work and the station whites but they followed him and found him at Kurinypirti and tied him to a horse's neck. Then they tied him to the horses' saddles with a chain, one kartiya on each side. They took him like that, making him walk between them. They took him back to the homestead and chained him up to a tree. I saw this happen at Limbunya. They tied him to a tree and took his clothes off. Before they beat him, they got the dogs and set them on him. The dogs ripped into him and tore him to shreds. There was blood everywhere. Then they got a stick and beat him around the head. They kept beating him until he had cuts all

round his head. And they got some wire and tied [it] to the end of a
whip and flogged him with that then. And you know how wire can
cut! (Jack survived the beating.) I was only a kid when I saw it happen. I saw these sorts of things happen as I was growing up ... some
kartiya had no compassion for ngumpin which is why they did that.

Jimmy Manngayarri

They camped the night, that lot of kartiya. Early in the morning
they ambushed people there and shot all the ngumpin there. They
shot the whole lot of them right there at the yards at Warluk. You
can go there and see where the yards are today. All around there,
where that waterhole is on the eastern side and waterlilies grow,
that's the place where it happened. They shot them there where that
yard is. Later it became a stock camp there for station workers. They
used to tell me this story: my grandfathers, great uncles, great
aunts, great-great grandparents and my father. I'm passing on here
what they told me. They shot everybody, perhaps on a sunny day
like today ... They had been killed like dogs from their own country. White people, with their violence and aggression, had come
down from Darwin and massacred people. They just left them
there, dead on the ground. The two men heaped up wood until
there was a large pyre. Then they dragged them one by one – an old
man ... another woman ... another man, dragging them across.
They threw them all on the fire and burnt them like dogs.

Ronnie Wavehill Wirrpngayarri

Wirrpngayarri's story ends as a parable of resistance, with Aboriginal men
spearing the two white men as they stand in front of the pyre. In 1967, the
petition signed in thumbprint by Vincent Lingiari and fellow leaders of the
Wave Hill walk-off mentioned that Seale Gorge held the remains of another

massacre, which took place nearby, at Tartarr. "This (Daguragu) is the main place of our dreaming only a few miles from the Seale Gorge where we have kept the bones of our martyrs all these years since white men killed many of our people," they wrote. "On the walls of the sacred caves where these bones are kept, are the paintings of the totems of our tribe."

> Further downstream from here, a large party of kartiya ambushed a group of our people. What was the reason for that? There was no reason. They hadn't killed any cattle; they were just out hunting kangaroos. But the kartiya were killing people all around here in every direction; they used to ambush them ... This story was told to me and I'm passing it on ... [People] went running through the bush: upstream, to the north and to the south through the scrub. They were shooting at people in the same way: old men, old women and children went running while the kartiya shot them. They didn't drag them across and burn them like at the other place; they heaped the bodies on top of each other and put them in a cave ... They just came like that and massacred Aboriginal people. They killed people everywhere. And what for? Because they found ngumpit in Australia, on this land ... there was too many people for them. It was terrible what they did. It's wrong.
>
> Ronnie Wavehill Wirrpngayarri

> They got one of the black trackers for policeman, so the black tracker used to come all the way up the Murray River and shooting up the Tully ... Most of the people fled back up to the hill and ... they got all the boys and the men one side, and the ladies and the girls over this other side of the place ... and shot 'em all ... Now, where you go to that place, the cattle still licking up whatever was there on the ground.
>
> Emily Murray

At another windmill – other side, Lipuru. Whitefellas shoot 'em. Kids and all. That's cruel, you know. Whitefellas came along, all the whitefellas, stock route blokes. Little boy – finish. Click, click, click … everywhere. How many funerals? One, two, three … Two men this side, wife and two kids other side.

Mavis Arnott

Our history is that our old people want to protect their country. Aalmara [whites] came and put up the flag. To our ancestors it was their country; they didn't understand what the flag meant. People came and stuck it there and they claimed it to be their country. But it wasn't; it was the people's country long before Aalmara came. This is their homeland, their dambeema; it should be recognised as their home. People came and claimed something that is not theirs. They don't want anybody interfering in their business. People fight for their country because it is theirs. They didn't fight with guns; they fought with a spear to protect their country.

Donny Wooladgoodja

Many of these stories have been told for generations in Aboriginal communities. Sometimes the details accord with evidence found in documentary sources, sometimes not. Corroborating evidence is not always at hand, often because settlers had long adopted a policy of dispensing brutal and summary forms of justice "quietly." Australians have yet to accept that they live in a country with two ways of knowing the past. Our hierarchies of storytelling dictate what we can and can't see. Documentary sources are accorded more authority and power. Indigenous testimony is more likely to be questioned and interrogated, its findings cast in doubt. This is another reason to hold a truth-telling commission: to hear and understand another way of knowing how Australia was founded and created. For Indigenous Australians, these stories are not "past." Taken as one living body of story, they form a mosaic that binds the historical experience of Aboriginal people from all parts of the continent. It is not the only tie, but it is one they want other Australians to hear more than any other. And it binds us all. Not as a vehicle for blame or guilt or a means to recoil in moral disgust and denounce the past. In order to understand what happened we have to step outside our own moral universe. History is not a trial of earlier generations, or of the present. The past matters because we give it life; because we seek to understand both its difference from the present and the traces of commonality that bind us to the lives of those who have gone before us. Until we listen to the voices of Indigenous Australians, we will continue to see the history of the country we share through European eyes.

The voices of delegates quoted in the Referendum Council's report stressed that the failure of recent federal governments to redress their grievances over the taking of their lands has its origins in a fundamental breach of faith that goes back to the late eighteenth century. As they pointed out, the Crown had made promises when it colonised Australia. In 1768, Captain Cook was instructed to take possession "with the consent of the natives." In 1787, Governor Phillip was instructed to treat the First Nations with "amity and kindness." Neither of these orders were obeyed. The name of James Cook features prominently in many of the statements made in the council's dialogues.

> Cook did not discover us, because we saw him. We were telling each other with smoke, yet in his diary, he said "discovered." (Torres Strait)

> Australia must acknowledge its history, its true history. Not Captain Cook. What happened all across Australia: the massacres and the wars. If that were taught in schools, we might have one nation, where we are all together. (Darwin)

> The invasion that started at Botany Bay is the origin of the funda-
> mental grievance between the old and new Australians: that Aus-
> tralia was colonised without the consent of its rightful owners.
> (Sydney)

Last year's fraught public debate over public memorials to our colonial founders appeared on the surface to be a debate about the wording of inscriptions, but was of course about something much deeper – the whole history of dispossession and how it should be publicly acknowledged. Of all the statues that were targeted, including those of Governor Lachlan Macquarie in Sydney, John Batman, the so-called founder of Melbourne, and the notorious "blackbirder" Robert Towns, after whom Townsville is named, one figure in particular provoked more controversy than any other: James Cook.

As we approach the 250th anniversary of Cook's landing at Kurnell in 2020, the story of the local community's attempts to commemorate the event reveals much about Australia's long struggle to come to terms with its past. No other patch of ground captures the dilemma of reconciling European and Indigenous histories in quite the same way.

The road cuts through a flat expanse of suburban homes as it heads towards the sea. Billboards along the way promise dream "beach lifestyles" in new housing estates that seem to stretch all the way to the horizon. Soon, shopping emporiums will tower above the dunes. It could be anywhere on Australia's coastal fringe. Except this place claims to be different. As the road approaches its destination, a weather-beaten sign hangs from an old metal post opposite an abandoned Caltex service station: "Welcome to Kurnell, the Birthplace of Modern Australia."

It's impossible to imagine a more unassuming site to announce contemporary Australia's beginnings. It appears as if someone erected the sign without asking, or perhaps left it there for the opening scene of a documentary film on a past civilisation. Kurnell Peninsula, on the southern shores of Botany Bay – the country of the Gweagal clan of the Dharawal nation – where James Cook came ashore in April 1770, is a place that most Australians have never visited, a national birthplace that citizens pass by.

I came to Kurnell late in 2017, only weeks after protesters had sprayed Cook's statue in Sydney's Hyde Park with graffiti, covering the original 1879 inscription – "Discovered this territory 1770" – with a blunt political message: "Change the date [of Australia Day]. No pride in genocide." Ever-keen to play the gallant patriot, and already angered by the decision of Melbourne's City of Yarra and Darebin councils to refuse to celebrate Australia Day on 26 January, Prime Minister Malcolm Turnbull rushed to condemn the vandalism as a "cowardly criminal act ... part of a deeply disturbing and totalitarian campaign to not just challenge our history but to deny it and obliterate it." Precisely who was in denial remains the question.

Stirred by the toppling of Confederate monuments across the United States, which had become a lightning rod for heated race debates, journalist and author Stan Grant penned a series of opinion pieces for the ABC, drawing attention to the cavernous silence in the words inscribed on Cook's statue in Hyde Park. "This statue speaks to emptiness," he proclaimed, "it speaks to our invisibility; it says that nothing truly mattered, nothing truly counted until a white sailor first walked on these shores." In the space of a few days the statue had been vandalised. Undeterred, Grant denounced the defacement as "disgraceful" but pressed home his point: the inscription was a lie. Aboriginal people had occupied the continent for over 60,000 years. Cook had no more discovered Australia than Bennelong had discovered England when he accompanied Governor Arthur Phillip to London in 1792.

Australia had been here before. The controversy over Cook's statue and other monuments to the colonial past raised the ghosts of the History Wars. Some saw a sinister new attempt to "rewrite history." Treasurer Scott Morrison took to the opinion pages of the *Australian*: "We don't get to choose when or how our story starts," he thundered, "or rewrite what has happened since ... [and] the same is true for nations." Thirty years after the deep divisions that marked the bicentenary in 1988, the country continued to circle the same old polarities: invasion or settlement? Frontier wars or occasional skirmishes? 26 January: a day for celebration or a day of mourning? Remarkably, to state publicly that James Cook did not discover Australia was still capable of causing controversy. Old verities die hard in this country.

All this Cook talk reminded me that I needed to make the trek to the place where he came ashore. Aside from vague recollections of being bussed there as a reluctant school student in the 1970s, I had visited the site, now situated in Kamay Botany Bay National Park, only once before. From the air, it appears a mere stone's throw from the city, but the journey by road offers the complete Sydney traffic experience. Early one afternoon, I drove the forty kilometres from Sydney's CBD to "the foot" – the name given in some Aboriginal stories to Kurnell Peninsula, the place where Cook's white feet apparently first touched land – to see the place for myself. What had been made of the history of Cook's landing at the site itself?

Before I arrived there, I was forced to pull over. I had not expected to see the sign. "Birthplace of modern Australia"? Such grandeur – the bold words inscribed on a rotting piece of wood hanging from a old pole. If there had been a birth, then it seemed that everyone had left town shortly afterwards. When was the sign erected? And by whom? I spoke to some locals, who had no idea. Others told me it had been there for as long as they could remember. After talking to members of the local historical society and Stephanie Bailey, the research librarian at Sutherland Shire Council, my search gained the support of a small army of willing researchers. All devotees of their local history, they wanted to know the provenance of the sign. Within days, we had the answer.

In June 1981, after months of vigorous campaigning by Sutherland Shire Council and the Kurnell community, NSW Labor premier Neville Wran directed the Sydney Cove Redevelopment Authority to remove all plaques in the Rocks that described the area as "Australia's birthplace." Labor MPs Mike Egan (Cronulla) and Bill Robb (Miranda) had managed to persuade Wran that the "honour of being the nation's birthplace" belonged solely to Kurnell. "Needless to say," Egan proudly told the NSW parliament, "there can only be one birthplace of the nation," and he would "hate to see a grave historical error perpetrated by the term being applied to some other area."

Once Wran decided on Kurnell, another problem arose. Having officially stripped the Rocks of its claim to be the "birthplace of the nation," what new epithet should be bestowed upon it? As a sop, the government announced that the Rocks would henceforth be known as the "cradle of the nation." Close enough to birth, perhaps, but still far enough away from suggesting that convicts founded the nation. As Egan reminded parliament: "At Sutherland Shire schools, it is taught that it was Captain Cook and not Captain Phillip who opened the way for British colonisation of Australia." Although the mere mention of "Botany Bay" had long been synonymous with convict depravity, Kurnell Peninsula's relative isolation from the site of the first penal settlement at Sydney Cove freed the Cook story from the convict stain. Fifteen kilometres as the crow flies was the distance between shame and pride.

After Wran's announcement, Sutherland Shire Council's sign-writer immediately set to work, erecting the new sign: "Welcome to the Birthplace of the Nation." But locals quickly pointed out that he had failed to mention Kurnell. He dutifully took the sign down and painted another, finally producing one to their satisfaction: "Welcome to Kurnell, birthplace of the nation." Residents were thrilled with the upgrade. Within three years of claiming the title, the first "Kurnell Historic Festival" to commemorate Cook's arrival at Botany Bay as the moment the nation was born took place, in 1984.

"Now tourists not only know where they are," boasted the local press, "but why they are there. And considering the state of Captain Cook Drive and the smells that sometimes emanate from the noxious industries lining the route to Australia's most sacred shrine, they might be wondering why they bothered." Ever since the 1950s, the jarring proximity of Kurnell's oil refineries to the nation's "birthplace" had seemed to mock the site's sacred status. Pollution and waste abounded. When Fairfax journalist Tracey Aubin visited the area shortly before the Bicentenary celebrations, she remarked that if Kurnell had "looked as bad in 1770," Cook would probably have "kept on sailing." Aubin found the streets "littered with as many pieces of rubbish as there are commemorations of the man." Not that environmental degradation at Kurnell was anything new. Thomas Holt, the wealthy wool merchant, financier and politician who purchased a massive estate at Botany Bay in 1861 and nine years later erected an obelisk in memory of Cook, his fellow Yorkshireman, had left a trail of environmental "enrichment" behind him. Holt released rabbits, cut down the vegetation that covered Kurnell's ancient sand dunes to graze cattle, then introduced foreign grasses in a desperate attempt to stabilise the dunes that had been decimated by his cattle and land clearing. In the twentieth century, sand mining continued the destruction, leaving lakes and waste dumps where dunes had once supported a delicately balanced ecosystem.

In the wake of the Bicentenary, Kurnell's claim to be the "birthplace of the nation" soon faltered for more profound reasons. In late 1993, shortly after the establishment of the Council for Aboriginal Reconciliation (1991) and the High Court's *Mabo* decision (1992), Sutherland Shire Council became uneasy about the possible "offence" that the sign might give to "many Aboriginal Australians." The nationwide "White Australia has a black history" campaign in 1988 – which culminated on 26 January in an all-night "survival" vigil in the sand hills at Kurnell – posed a question that remains unanswered: how to celebrate the birth of a nation that has dispossessed and excluded its first peoples? At the same time, the depth of Aboriginal occupation of the continent was becoming more widely known. Words that appeared only ten years earlier as cause for triumphant celebration were now seen as offensive and misleading. As Mayor Ian Swords told Sutherland Shire Council in November 1993:

> For some time, I have been conscious of the fact that the term currently used by Council, "Birthplace of the Nation," causes offence to many Aboriginal Australians. This is not surprising, as this expression infers that no civilisation existed in Australia before the arrival of Captain Cook at Kurnell in 1770 ... I would like to propose to Council that it replace its existing slogan with "Birthplace of Modern Australia."

This term both preserves a reference to the landing in 1770 in Australian history and, at the same time, removes the offensive and inaccurate inference that no civilisation existed before Captain Cook.

Sword's motion was passed unanimously. Visitors to Kurnell would now be welcomed to the "birthplace of modern Australia." Although the reason for the change was stated in the council's minutes, it was largely hidden from public view. The existence of Aboriginal "civilisation" had forced the change in wording, yet, typically, that same civilisation was not mentioned. Twenty-five years later, the sign still stands. Just.

I later discovered that the story went back even further than 1981. "For years" before 1981 (probably from around the time Captain Cook Drive was opened in 1954), a sign "graced the entrance" to the suburb, welcoming visitors to the "birthplace of Australia." It was a telling succession of changes: from the "birthplace of Australia" to the "birthplace of the nation" and, finally, "the birthplace of modern Australia." I thought of Malcom Turnbull's knee-jerk response to the suggestion that Cook's statue in Hyde Park be removed or changed, working up a patriotic lather – "This is the greatest country in the world, our achievement is so remarkable" – and professing his horror at the idea that we should "go round rewriting history, editing statues, changing the inscriptions … deleting Australia Day." "I mean, what are these people thinking?" he bellowed. Presumably they were thinking along similar lines to the people who had edited the sign at Kurnell over successive generations – altering public signs to claim the mantle of the nation's "birthplace," then making subtle but significant shifts in the wording of inscriptions as they reconsidered the past in light of new knowledge. Since when have we not been "rewriting history"?

*

From 1822 – when an old Aboriginal man reportedly led members of Sydney's Philosophical Society to Cook's landing place and a brass plaque was fixed to a nearby cliff-face proclaiming that "these shores were discovered ... under the auspices of British science" – commemorations of Cook's presence on Australian soil have shifted constantly: all the way from polite indifference to boastful declarations of Britain's "undisputed possession" of the "entire continent." In 1870 Cook's landing was acknowledged as "the centenary of British possession"; one hundred years later, Aboriginal protesters across the bay at La Perouse, the site of Sydney's oldest surviving Aboriginal community, wore blood-red headbands and threw wreaths into the sea. For both Aboriginal and non-Aboriginal Australians, Cook has become the anvil on which stories of possession and dispossession have been struck.

In the wake of Federation, when a pantheon of national heroes was sorely needed, a concerted attempt was made to establish Cook as Australia's Columbus. NSW MP John Perry claimed that Cook had "given us this country in trust," as if the few days he spent at Botany Bay in 1770 had miraculously delivered a whole continent to Britain in one fell swoop. Estate agents sold new housing sites extolling the site's historic value: "Be Patriotic – own a Portion of the Birthplace of Australia." In the earnest kitsch of historical re-enactments, Cook was endlessly arriving. His departure, or what happened before or after the handful of days he spent at Botany Bay, mattered little, let alone the fact that he stayed far longer at the Endeavour River on the Cape York Peninsula than he did at Botany Bay. Forcing his way ashore, he commanded the beginning of British civilisation with the wave of his hand, like Moses parting the waters of the Red Sea.

At the inaugural national commemoration of Cook's landing in 1901, an "old hulk" was anchored in the bay about 200 metres offshore. In case onlookers were in any doubt regarding the vessel's identity, the word *Endeavour* was "crudely painted" on the ship's exterior. Ashore, a group of "Queensland Aboriginals" stood "decorated in their tribal war paint," trained, as one observer remarked, to "personify the barbarity of their habits." They had been brought more than a thousand kilometres by their "protector," Archibald Meston, to play the Gweagal – colourful ornaments of what was thought to be a dying culture. Their retreat before

Cook's musket-fire, graphically emphasised in the re-enactment, implicitly represented their disappearance from the nation that Cook had apparently spawned.

Yet few of these carefully scripted and choreographed displays stirred the emotions of the Australian people, most of whom lived thousands of kilometres from Kurnell, in states with their own founding moments. Even at the 150th anniversary of Cook's landing, in 1920, the story had already been eclipsed by the loss of more than 60,000 Australian lives in World War I. Now Cook was depicted not only as the man who "discovered" Australia but also as the father of the Anzacs, delivering white men to Antipodean shores so that their children's children would one day return to Europe to die for the Empire. As the Sydney Mail explained, Cook's arrival in 1770 led to Australia leaving "thousands of her dead on the battlefields of Europe to cement and sanctify the bond between the Old World and the youngest of the Earth's nations."

For all these myriad incarnations, the dream that the story of Cook's landing would "stir the blood of Australians" and lead to Kurnell becoming a "Mecca for millions of tourists" has never taken hold. In 1909, when a tourist pamphlet boasted that "what Plymouth Rock is to America" Kurnell would soon become for Australia, it admitted in the same breath that the place was "little known and certainly little reverenced." In coming years, steamers and ferries brought small numbers of tourists from La Perouse. Local Aboriginal people entertained them with stories of their people's resistance to Cook's landing, sold souvenirs and demonstrated boomerang-throwing. As shanty towns sprang up on the northern and southern shores of Botany Bay during the Depression, the image of a largely forgotten outpost proved hard to shake. At the time of the nation's sesquicentenary, in 1938, journalists described "cave dwellers" living "along the ocean cliffs" and a handful of "settlers" pushing their car-tyred drays on a "rutted bumpy track" through a maze of "wilderness and scrub." "Is there any place in the world," the local press asked forlornly, "which would allow its national birthplace to be [so] neglected?"

For the Gweagal of Botany Bay, who had resisted Cook's landing in 1770 – two warriors raising their spears in defiance, before Cook fired his musket on three separate occasions, injuring one man and forcing his way ashore as two spears were thrown at him – Cook did not give birth to modern Australia so much as spawn the idea that Australia was Britain's for the taking; a place where "the natives" were not "very numerous" and lived "in small parties" along the coast. Displaying the "English colours" on shore each day, Cook carved the date and name of his ship in a tree at Kurnell and sailed northwards, claiming possession of the "whole Eastern coast" of the continent and naming it "New South Wales." Weeks later, reflecting on his encounter with the Gweagal, he admitted that "all they seem'd to want was for us to be gone," words that were subsequently quoted so often that they became prophetic. For Aboriginal people across the continent in the years ahead, Cook's name came to stand for all white invaders. He was the first of them and he was all of them – a series of happenings both past and present – more a body of story than a man.

*

As I drove on towards the visitors' centre, the slightly tilted "Welcome" sign receding fast behind me, I wondered how these starkly different understandings of Cook – everything from the purveyor of scientific knowledge and British law to the progenitor of "modern Australia" through to the embodiment of invasion and dispossession – could possibly be reconciled. The bitter dispute over the Cook monument in Hyde Park gave little grounds for hope. But I soon discovered there was a vast chasm separating this shrill national debate from what had been achieved on the ground at Kurnell. As with so many other examples of social and political change in Australia, the parliament has lagged far behind the people. While the Turnbull government and tabloid media reacted defensively – vigorously protecting Cook's legacy and attacking those who wanted his statue in Hyde Park removed or altered – local communities at Kurnell had found a way to move beyond the tired polarities of the culture and history wars.

In April 1995, shortly before the 225th anniversary of Cook's landing, Sutherland Shire's mayor, Genevieve Rankin, consulted Dharawal elders. They told her that they would find the sight of an *Endeavour* replica in Botany Bay "distressing" and "offensive." They also planned protests for the day of commemoration. In an effort to conciliate them, Rankin offered to deliver an official apology at the ceremony. But when the press reported that she would offer an apology for "Koori genocide by early settlers," the Council erupted in controversy and readers contacted the local press to complain. Their reasons prefigured those offered by Prime Minister John Howard two years later, in his response to the *Bringing Them Home* report on the Stolen Generations: "we are personally not responsible." They objected vehemently to any attempt to apologise for the crimes of the early settlers. The celebrations should go ahead, they insisted, without being "hijacked" by special interest groups. Caught in the crossfire, Rankin decided that she would speak only for herself, offering her "personal" apology for the "attempted genocide and dispossession of Australia's indigenous peoples." The protests went ahead in any case. Elder Les Davison insisted his people were "not celebrating." Instead, across the bay at La Perouse, they threw wreaths into the sea and lowered the Aboriginal flag.

The impasse at Kurnell – which mirrored the stand-off that had divided the Bicentenary celebrations in 1988 – would last in one form or another until 1999, when NSW Tourism announced "a marketing effort to capitalise on the area's history from a European and indigenous perspective," positioning Kurnell as a "unique cultural meeting place." By the next commemoration of Cook's landing, Dharawal elders and council officials had agreed to hold the ceremony under a new banner: "Meeting of Two Cultures." Other changes quickly followed. In 2000, seven years after Sutherland Shire Council modified the "Welcome" sign at Kurnell in a gesture of reconciliation, Kurnell Parkland was renamed "Kamay Botany Bay

National Park." In 2003, the spirit of this shared name was cemented when Cook's landing site was renamed the "Meeting Place Precinct" and Sutherland Shire Council formally exchanged "reconciliation statements" with Dharawal elders. Since 2000, every anniversary of Cook's landing has been commemorated through a "Meeting of Two Cultures" ceremony, in which visiting dignitaries, politicians, local Indigenous elders and school and community groups come together to listen, remember and share their understandings of Cook's visit. Aboriginal, Australian and Sutherland Shire flags fly side-by-side. It has not been without difficulty. Some Dharawal elders have expressed their dissatisfaction with aspects of the ceremony directly to the Council. At the same time, the goodwill and determination to resolve these differences is undeniable.

At the ceremony in 2012, local schoolchildren sang the national anthem in the Dharawal language. Days earlier, Kurnell adopted a new flag which saw the Dharawal whale totem positioned beside the silhouette of a tall ship – imagine a new Australian flag that incorporated Indigenous symbols. It was a far cry from the shrieking and wailing about history in the house on Capital Hill.

When federal Liberal MP Bruce Baird joined the ceremony in 2000, he revealed that in 1956, as a student at Sutherland High School, he had taken part in a re-enactment of Cook's landing. While some of his friends per-formed as members of Cook's landing party, Baird played one of "the natives." The practice of "blacking up" white actors to play the Gweagal continued well into the 1960s. It would take nearly five decades to under- stand why it was necessary to leave this kind of demeaning pageantry behind. Although few in number, monuments to white Australia's pride in Cook had dominated the area near the landing site for nearly two centuries.

When one speaks to people in the Sutherland Shire today, it's clear that Cook's story still commands enormous pride and respect. His stately image has graced the council's logo in one form or another since 1906. He seems to get larger and more mysterious with every passing year. The story of his time at Botany Bay in 1770 has become so layered and multifarious that his afterlife can't be pinned down.

Remarkably, in 2015, the Dharawal set eyes for the first time on the stolen bark shield that their ancestors had used to defend themselves against Cook's musket fire. Brought to Canberra from the British Museum, where it had probably found its way after Cook and Banks returned to England, it was one of the prize artefacts in the National Museum's *Encounters* exhibition. The shield captured the imagination of visitors more than almost any other object on display. Its dark, furrowed patina and formidable symmetry seemed to hold the secrets of the entire cross-cultural encounter. Its power was undeniable. Was the small, perfectly formed hole in the middle of the shield a viewing-hole, caused by a "single pointed lance," as Banks described the hole in one shield, or a bullet hole caused by Cook's musket fire, as claimed by some Dharawal elders today? Could this really be the same shield that Cook and Banks took with them when they left Botany Bay in May 1770? Perhaps. Made from red "mangrove wood growing along the coast at least five hundred kilometres north of Sydney," it provided graphic evidence of the vast extent of Indigenous trade networks. Elder Shayne Williams described it as "our national treasure," a shield that "represents a whole history of this country" and "all Aboriginal people" because it embodies "Aboriginal resistance," both in 1770 and in the twenty-first century. Reflecting on the "spiritual" and emotional feelings the shield gave rise to, Williams admitted that he was "sort of grateful that they were taken and preserved ... because not much has been preserved of any artefacts within the Sydney Basin."

In the months during and after the exhibition, the story of the shield continued to unfold. Rodney Kelly, who claimed to be a sixth-generation descendant of one of the two Gweagal warriors who opposed Cook's landing in 1770, led a well-publicised campaign for the shield and spears stolen from his ancestors to be repatriated. By late 2016 he had the support of both the Senate and the NSW Parliament. To date, both the British

Museum and Cambridge University's Museum of Archaeology and Anthropology, which holds many of the spears, have refused to hand them back. Disappointed but not deterred, Kelly continued his investigation elsewhere. Visiting several other institutions in Europe with large collections of Indigenous artefacts, he made a surprise discovery in Berlin's Ethnological Museum. In a handwritten catalogue from the late eighteenth century he found an entry for items collected at "Botany Bay 1770." When museum curators retrieved them, Kelly was astonished. It was another Gweagal shield and a boomerang marked with the telltale Gweagal "zigzag" patterns, both of which were apparently brought to Berlin in the early nineteenth century after being purchased at a London auction. Until Kelly made the discovery, the shield's existence was unknown, a reminder that so many of the Indigenous artefacts held in museum collections overseas – the British Museum alone holds over 6000 items – remain unidentified and unseen by their rightful owners.

Given the transformation of Cook's landing site in recent years, the old "Welcome" sign at the entrance to Kurnell should be pulled down before it falls down. A new sign should be erected in keeping with the spirit of the annual commemoration of Cook's landing: "Welcome to Kurnell: Where Cultures Meet." To suggest that Cook's landing at Botany Bay gave birth to "modern Australia" is to leave Indigenous culture exactly where white Australia has long preferred to cast it – as "ancient," "traditional" and "pre-modern" – bands of men and women who wandered the country in search of their daily subsistence, waiting for history to begin. "Modern Australia" was (and is) created as much by Aboriginal people as by the invaders and their descendants and all those who have come after them.

The name for Cook's landing spot – "Inscription Point" – embodies the dilemma, overwriting Indigenous histories with the possessive stamp of British civilisation. James Cook's eight days at Botany Bay have been made to appear more significant than millennia of Indigenous occupation. So many of the attitudes that drove the colonisation of Australia remain embedded in the language we use today – in our placenames, our descriptions of the land, our political priorities, our constitution and our national anthem – that we have only just begun to see that this country was "inscribed" long before Europeans knew of its existence.

As for Cook's statue in Hyde Park and other monuments to our colonial past, surely it would be more productive to add to them rather than erase them from the landscape. If we explain why the original inscriptions were written, and why we no longer accept them as credible or the whole story, we transform the platitudes, historical fallacies and heroic figures associated with our public statues into sites of learning and reflection. No longer merely ornamental, they suddenly become useful. If we fail to do this, then we fail the most basic test of the challenge of recognition: to change the way we see our history.

In Cooktown, where Cook spent seven weeks repairing the *Endeavour* in 1770 and met fierce resistance after his crew hauled a dozen giant green sea turtles on deck and refused to share them with "the natives," local elder and historian Alberta Hornsby and Loretta Sullivan, president of the Cooktown Re-enactment Association, are preparing to commemorate his eventual rapprochement with the Guugu Yimithirr as "the first moment of reconciliation in Australia's history." Angered by several men who'd set fire to the grass where he'd left a "forge and a sow and a litter of young pigs," Cook fired his musket, wounding an Aboriginal man, after which the men immediately retreated. Seizing the spears that they had left behind, Cook and Banks were approached about an hour later by "a little old man" carrying a spear "without a point," with several men brandishing spears walking only a few metres behind him. As he walked towards them, the old man halted several times, "collecting moisture from under his armpit with his finger" and drawing it "through his mouth." Cook and Banks "beckoned him" to come closer. At this point, the old man turned to his comrades, who "laid their lances against a tree." Then, slowly, they all came forward to meet one another. After they exchanged gifts and greetings, Cook returned their spears, remarking later in his journal that this seemed to have "reconciled everything." More than two hundred years later, Alberta Hornsby and her late uncle, Eric Deeral, explained the story through Guugu Yimithirr law: how the old man, by drawing sweat from under his armpits and "blowing the sweat on his hands into the air," was performing a ritual known as "ngalangundaama," a call for "protection and calm." In Guugu Yimithirr law, no blood was to be spilt on "Waymburr," the land on which Cook had come ashore and fired his musket. At last it was possible to understand the old man's gesture of reconciliation from the perspective of the Guugu Yimithirr; it was a request for his law to be honoured and calm to be restored. For Alberta and Loretta, the story represents an inspiring moment of reconciliation, which they hope will form the centrepiece of Cooktown's celebrations for the 250th anniversary of Cook's visit.

The Kurnell and Cooktown communities' willingness to rethink the way they commemorate Cook's landing shows how productive acknowledging the past can be. By moving away from the tired clichés of discovery and nation-making that once dominated, they have made Cook a more promising emissary. In stark contrast, it is the federal government, with its absurd claims of "Stalinist interference," that appears fearful and defensive. For as long as we refuse to relinquish the triumphalist and monovocal view of our past, we seal ourselves off from understanding history as anything other than a crude choice between shame and pride.

In all the stories that have circled around James Cook since he stepped ashore at Botany Bay in April 1770 — the assertions of historical firsts, the fierce disputations over Cook's statue and the countless ex post facto claims freighted onto the shoulders of one brilliant navigator from Yorkshire — it's possible to witness a nation hankering for a foundation narrative and its dispossessed people demanding that they be included in that same story on just terms. As the ways of remembering Cook's landings have changed over time, he has become much more than the embodiment of modernity, invasion and dispossession; he is also the promise of peace and reconciliation. He plants the seeds and is gone. He claims possession without consent, yet he also brings with him the law that will belatedly recognise native title more than two centuries later. He is at once the agent of destruction and the agent of redemption. A man who becomes a story that remains open-ended – a story that continually draws us back, although we know the whole tale will always elude us. Cook can be lionised, misrepresented and reviled, but he can never be banished from Australia's historical consciousness. We stand forever on the beach with him.

In September 2016, Warren Foster, a Djiringanj man from Wallaga Lake, on the south coast of New South Wales, spoke at a gathering of local historians and writers in Bega. A dancer, musician, teacher and writer, Foster walked nonchalantly up to the podium, picked up a marker and wrote one word on the whiteboard: "HISTORY." Then he added a slash to it: "HIS/STORY."

"History is his story," he said forcefully, "not our story ... Jimmy Cook! We were watching him. All the way up the coast. We were watching him. He named our Gulaga Mount Dromedary."

By now, the audience was in his hand. He drew a horizontal line, then placed notches at regular intervals until he had a timeline. "This is your history," he said. "First Cook, then this, then that. We don't use this!" Another long pause. He drew a large circle and wrote two words inside – "dreaming" and "law." There was a collective murmur of recognition from the audience. But Foster wasn't done yet. "This circle is one time," he avowed. "This circle is our history. In this, there is no time. There is only Dreamtime. Every time we tell stories we are in one time." As he continued, it became clear to everyone in the room how far removed their understanding of history was from Foster's. While they thought of history as a succession of happenings, a relentless march forwards from past to present marked with key events or "memories," Foster had shown them that this was yet another colonial imposition. Along with every other aspect of British culture, including government and law, "History" disembarked with "Jimmy Cook" at Botany Bay.

Later, answering questions from the floor, Foster reflected with considerable regret that non-Indigenous Australians remained largely ignorant of Indigenous forms of knowledge. "You just don't know," he insisted, "you don't understand how we live." He admitted that he still felt like an "outsider" in his own country. Foster had heard many whitefellas speak of acknowledging history and "moving on," as if the past was a commodity that could be selectively embraced and abandoned at the nation's convenience. But he was unable to leave history behind him. He lived its consequences every day.

His comments reminded me of a remark by Warlpiri elder Rosie Nappurrula. When the Europeans came to her land in Central Australia, she said, it represented "the end of the Jukurrpa [Dreaming]." This was not to say that the Dreaming was over, but that she was unable to live in the Dreaming in the same way as before. As Peggy Rockman Napaljarri and Lee Cataldi explain in their introduction to *Warlpiri Dreamings and Histories*, an extraordinary collection of fifteen stories from Warlpiri elders, the arrival of Europeans meant the "end of the Jukurrpa as a world view, as a single, total explanation for the universe."

If this is true of blackfella Dreaming, what then of whitefella Dreaming? After nearly 230 years of living with Indigenous Australians, has it not too been altered? Now that the Indigenous cultures that were thought to be destined for extinction have emerged to demand their rightful place in the Commonwealth, and in light of new historical knowledge, can we continue living in our Dreaming in the same way as before? With our gods, laws, institutions and beliefs unchanged? Still asserting that the country is ours for the taking? Still believing that our civilisation has a right to supercede that of Indigenous Australians? Still claiming that our ways of governing the country are superior and uncontestable? While Australians today embrace aspects of Indigenous culture in ways that would have been unimaginable only fifty years ago, and while our communities show an increasing willingness to listen to Indigenous voices and stories, the state lags far behind. As history's victor, the Commonwealth has yet to give a true indication that whitefella Dreaming has changed, that it is willing to concede something more than the warm inner glow of comforting words and good feelings. Symbolic recognition alone is an impoverished vision. After little more than two centuries of European occupation, we agree to say to the people whose ancestors have lived here for thousands of generations, "We recognise you!" It's precisely for this reason that the Uluru Statement called for "substantive constitutional change and structural reform." Without this, "Recognition" is a hollow vessel that soothes the conscience of whitefellas but does nothing to improve the lives of Indigenous Australians.

Recent Commonwealth governments have failed to rise to the challenge of substantial reform, not only in Indigenous affairs, but across a wide range of policy areas. Political journalists rightly complain about the lack of "narrative." At a quite fundamental level, we have failed to appreciate the scale and opportunity of the challenge; to conceive of "substantive structural reform" as a web of interconnected aspirations, and to express these powerfully, as an overarching statement of the nation's direction. This is much more than nostalgia for Keating's "big picture"; rather, it is a disillusioned electorate's expectation of government that continues to go unheeded. Between 1996 and 2007, John Howard steadfastly refused to embrace reconciliation except within the narrow limits of his own partisan agenda. Rudd's ascendancy brought the Apology and briefly offered hope, but since his dramatic political execution in 2010, our federal politics has struggled to rise above the thin theatre of leadership rivalries and petty political point-scoring. Bitterly divided major parties – their internal ideological battles often more fiercely contested than those fought with their political opponents – poll-driven politics, feverish media speculation and narrow parliamentary majorities have not helped. The capacity of our political leaders to step back and take the long view has been continually undermined, often by their own actions. We have had no shortage of leaders but find little evidence of leadership. The Turnbull government has not taken up the invitation to "walk with" Indigenous Australians towards "a better future." It has also rejected the most visionary political document to emerge in the last decade. The Uluru Statement from the Heart may have been "circulated" around the corridors of Parliament House but its potential still waits to be realised.

> Our Aboriginal and Torres Strait Islander tribes were the first sovereign Nations of the Australian continent and its adjacent islands ...

> This sovereignty is a spiritual notion: the ancestral tie between the land, or "mother nature" ... With substantive constitutional change and structural reform, we believe this ancient sovereignty can shine through as a fuller expression of Australia's nationhood.

Australians have long lacked confidence in their civilisation. Deeply ashamed until the 1970s of our convict ancestry and colonial origins, forever measuring our society and culture against superior British and European models, endlessly "coming of age" or pining for prominence on an imagined "world stage" while our political leaders shrilly proclaim that we live in "the greatest country in the world" — we have long preferred self-congratulation to criticism. In this respect, we are not exceptional. Yet the most profound source of our alienation from the continent remains to be fully appreciated and overcome. Until the late twentieth century, white Australia was intent on conquering, eradicating and forgetting Indigenous Australia. We believed that history began in 1770 on the shores of Botany Bay. We were not only estranged from the history of the country's violent foundation on the frontier, we were also completely disconnected from the "spiritual" and "ancient sovereignty" of Aboriginal people. This too was something we sought to overcome, or reduce to the level of superstition and fairytale. Now the Uluru Statement asks us to confirm that we have overturned our assumptions — not only about the beginning of "history," but also about our relationship with the country and our identity as a people. It is both an invitation and a challenge: to embrace the ancient sovereignty that we have long denied and finally allow it to form the bedrock of our nation's identity. After all that has happened since 1770, this is a gift of incalculable generosity. And it speaks directly to key elements of the new constitutional settlement we are attempting to establish in the years ahead: recognition, the republic and truth-telling.

The Uluru Statement's invitation to ground the Commonwealth's sovereignty in the ancient sovereignty of Indigenous Australia goes to the heart of the coming republic. Since the late nineteenth century, when Henry Lawson and the *Bulletin* argued that Australia should "cut the painter" and sever its ties with the United Kingdom, republicans have always imagined that their independence would come from severance alone. The entire argument about independence was built on breaking away from Britain. In the 1960s and 1970s, Donald Horne argued that retaining our links with the British monarchy entrenched the idea of Australia as a derivative society and fostered a culture of psychological inferiority and dependence on others. The path to a more confident and independent Australia could only be built by turning away from Britain and the monarchy. By the 1990s, the argument for a republic was not so much about Britain – republicans argued that they wanted to retain Australia's British heritage and parliamentary traditions – as it was about an Australian head of state. It was the nationality of our head of state – even more than the antiquated and undemocratic nature of hereditary monarchy – that drove the argument for a republic. Yet for all this time, republicans have imagined that the question of the country's independence was anchored solely in its relationship with Britain and her monarchy. We have looked outwards rather than within, knowing what we want to reject but being less certain about what we want to create in the monarchy's absence. "Business as usual" – the credo of minimalist republicanism in the 1990s – is no longer a credible response. Nor will royal rigor mortis set us free. In 2018, the republic has little to do with our relationship with Britain or the monarchy. We have already "broken away" and become an independent nation except in two crucial respects: we are without an Australian head of state and we have yet to *anchor* our vision of popular sovereignty in the continent's Indigenous antiquity, as the Uluru Statement from the Heart invites us to do. This is the true source of a more mature and independent Australia – the grounding of our sovereignty on our own soil, in the songlines and histories of an ancient island continent.

One of the many questions that historian Manning Clark asked about Australia – he seemed to spend as much time contemplating the country's future as he did writing its past – was whether Indigenous Australians, Australians of British origin and those who have come to this country from more than 150 countries around the world would find a way to build a new "civilisation" – one that Clark believed would be not only independent, republican and genuinely inclusive, but also fiercely protective of its environment, fully reconciled with its past and completely *at home*. As someone who wondered often if he "truly belonged" in Australia, Clark saw the connection between the "spirit of place" and a new vision of popular sovereignty. In 2012, novelist Kim Scott pointed to the same connection from a different perspective: "This is an Aboriginal nation," he asserted. "It's a black country, the continent. Some people are starting to think about [whether we can] graft a contemporary Australian community onto its Indigenous roots." Naturally, neither Scott, who has done much to preserve his Noongar language and culture, nor the authors of the Uluru Statement, are implying that we should simply appropriate the "ancient sovereignty" of Indigenous Australians in a latter-day form of colonial theft. What they are suggesting is that this process of "grafting" can only avoid appropriation if it is accompanied by a constitutional settlement that brings a fundamental realignment of the relationship between Indigenous Australians and the state. For every Australian citizen, regardless of their ethnicity, a meaningful constitutional settlement with Indigenous Australia would stand as a fundamental pillar of the democratic nation to which they belong. Truth-telling is the other cornerstone.

The reasons why are spelt out in the Referendum Council's report. "Now is an opportunity for the First Nations to tell the truth about history in our own voices and from our own point of view. And for mainstream Australians to hear those voices and to reconsider what they know and understand about their nation's history. This will be challenging, but the truth about invasion needs to be told." Council members stressed how delegates repeatedly emphasised the need for non-Aboriginal Australians to "take responsibility for that history and this legacy it has created." These demands have still not registered in the corridors of Parliament House or in the broader community. The experience of post-apartheid South Africa's Truth and Reconciliation Commission (1996–98), and Canada's more recent Truth and Reconciliation Commission (2008–15), which inquired into the forced removal of Indigenous children to "residential schools," demonstrated the capacity of truth-telling commissions to promote "healing and restorative truth." I hope that an Australian commission would involve both Aboriginal and non-Aboriginal truth-tellers. As Inga Clendinnen explained in 2009, the purpose of truth-telling is not to "wring our hands over past brutalities and injustices," but, in Australia's case, to understand how punitive expeditions, which were often composed of a majority of Aboriginal Native Police, were sent out and did their work. Berating Australians, besmirching what they perceive as an honourable past, or telling them that they must know the truth of their history without explaining why can be counterproductive. Asking them to listen to Indigenous voices in good faith holds out more hope of change.

Already at a local level, community groups (including the descendants of families involved on both sides) have come together on the anniversaries of massacres such as Coniston, Myall Creek and Ravensthorpe to erect memorials, commemorate the tragic events and listen to one another's stories. They are all inspiring examples of truth-telling and healing that will prove invaluable for a future national body. As ever, governments have yet to catch up. While every state parliament has passed an act of "recognition" (Victoria was the first, in 2004), few of these reassuring declarations have confronted the reality of violent dispossession and almost all are accompanied by "no legal effect" clauses. More importantly, there is no state-sanctioned memorial to the frontier wars in Australia. This absence is one of the most telling "silences" that continues to reign over our "official" historical imagination. Our federal governments have not been able to acknowledge the truth of the country's violent foundation. While they busily erect memorials to our servicemen and women who fought in conflicts overseas – Canberra's Anzac Parade, with its ever-burgeoning number of war memorials, already resembles the worst of Soviet-era bombast – they refuse to acknowledge the Aboriginal patriots who died defending their country. After a truth-telling commission which allowed the nation to understand the historical perspective of Indigenous Australians, a national memorial to the frontier wars would not only be the next logical step, it would have more force. It would also act as a sorely needed corrective in other ways.

Anzac Day, which has become Australia's de facto national day, is a case in point. Unlike any other nation, Australia has embraced a legend of national birth that takes place 16,000 kilometres offshore. Not on our own soil but on the distant shores of the Gallipoli Peninsula in Turkey. In the surfeit of Anzac literature, we often fail to ask the most important question of all: why have we rushed to embrace an event that took place so far away from this country as our key founding moment? By doing so, we've turned our eyes from the true site of melancholy, loss and "birth" in our history, the land itself – and the encounter between Aboriginal people and those who came from across the seas to claim this land. The timing of Anzac Day's resurgence – which began in earnest after more than a decade's debate over the Bicentenary, Mabo and the Stolen Generations – was not coincidental. For conservatives especially, exasperated by the rise of black armband history, 25 April offered a much more attractive proposition: a foundational narrative that told of heroic sacrifice and the loss of *honourable* blood, conveniently situated far away from the site of the country's true foundation. Our excessive emotional investment in Anzac Day – our governments go to extraordinary lengths to repatriate the bodies of our soldiers buried in unmarked graves on the former battlefields of the Western Front in France, yet show little interest in the repatriation of the bodies of Aboriginal warriors, many of them "unknown" and sent back to England during the frontier wars – points yet again to our inability to mourn the dispossession of Aboriginal people. In a very real way, we have continued to circumnavigate the heart of the matter.

The fracas about the future of Australia Day – the chorus demanding the date be changed, which gets louder every year – would also take on a different inflection. The voices heard in the commission would speak directly to the point of division: invasion and dispossession. After the Indigenous perspective on Australia's history was aired in such a way, the question of Australia Day – which has, after all, only been a national public holiday since 1994 – would be more easily settled. There seems little point in changing the date until we have a viable alternative. Rather than choosing another day, the day needs to choose itself. We need to first prepare the ground for a truly unifying national day by working through the challenges of constitutional recognition, truth-telling and genuine legislative reform. This could happen in a way that changes the nature of commemoration on 26 January, making it more inclusive, or lead to another date entirely. In any case, it is difficult to imagine that Australia Day can survive in its current form. How can we continue to pretend that 26 January represents a genuinely inclusive and unifying national day when it is patently a day of such painful memories for Indigenous Australians?

As it stands, the day is already untethered from the events that took place on 26 January 1788, when Governor Arthur Phillip and his officers, who had already been in Sydney Harbour since 21 January, came ashore to plant the British flag and toast the King. By placing Australia Day on the 26th we have not chosen the date of the First Fleet's arrival on the east coast of Australia – the first ships arrived at Botany Bay on 18 January – nor the date of the reading of the royal commission, 7 February 1788, when Phillip addressed the marines and convicts. Instead, in a direct affront to Indigenous Australians, whose "ancient sovereignty" we have still not acknowledged, we have chosen the day of flag-planting and the assertion of sovereignty by the British Crown, which also happens to be the anniversary of the massacre at Waterloo Creek in 1838, when up to fifty Kamilaroi people were killed in the New England District of New South Wales. Little of this is mentioned when we celebrate Australia Day.

The focus is on citizenship ceremonies and, as the cliché goes, "the things that unite Australians rather than those that divide us." Even the convicts and Phillip struggle for airplay, which explains why less than half those polled in two recent surveys could connect Australia Day with the arrival of the First Fleet.

Eager to depict themselves as defenders of the national honour, politicians – including Malcolm Bligh Turnbull – line up to trumpet the day as an occasion when we should be "proud of Australia and its history and celebrate all of our achievements." After ABC's Triple J moved its annual "Hottest 100" from Australia Day to 27 January, the *Australian*'s editorial followed the politicians' lead, absurdly claiming that Triple J was attempting to "subvert the nation." Laying the grounds for another culture war will only prove counterproductive. We desperately need a more enlightened approach – a way of facing up to the true history of the country's foundation without condemning European Australia as irredeemable or dismissing the violence of dispossession. As Waleed Aly perceptively remarked in April 2016, "as a nation, we lack a national mythology that can cope with our shortcomings. That transforms our historical scars into fatal psychological wounds, leaving us with a bizarre need to insist everything was – and is – as good as it gets." A truth-telling commission might well allow us to find a path towards that elusive national mythology, one in which the legitimacy, "equitable sovereignty" and "equal custodianship" of both Aboriginal and non-Aboriginal Australia are acknowledged and celebrated. At the very least, it will provide Indigenous Australians with an exceptional forum within which to tell their stories. For once, the eyes and ears of the entire nation will be upon them.

In the national capital's Parliamentary Triangle, where this essay began, the silences echo even more loudly. If Canberra is where the nation becomes brick and mortar, then there is a missing piece of architecture. In 2014, a federal government committee recommended that a National Keeping Place be erected in the Parliamentary Triangle. It would house "Aboriginal and Torres Strait Islander ancestral remains with no known community of origin." It would also "serve as a memorial dedicated to the memory of all ancestors who were removed from their traditional homelands, including those that may never be repatriated from collections" around the world. The Yawuru elder and National Museum Council member Peter Yu put the case for a Keeping Place more succinctly than anyone before or since. "A national keeping place," he said:

> would also be a centre for learning and for me it would become like a beacon of conscience in the national capital where it reminds us of the importance of history and what we can do to each other, but [also] where we can learn from what we've done to each other. One of the problems with Australia is that we don't really recognise the true history of the country. It was a brutal history. And I think that contemporarily most Australians are divorced from understanding the trauma in that history.

The natural place for a Keeping Place lies waiting near Reconciliation Place, on the grassy mound between Parliament House and Lake Burley Griffin, in the central axis that connects the Parliament to the Australian War Memorial. It is also the appropriate place to build a National Memorial – a free-standing monument positioned in the heart of the national capital – dedicated to the memory of all those who died in the frontier wars. If we imagine the Parliamentary Triangle as international visitors might see it, the absence of such a memorial and a National Keeping Place – which could be both a place of reflection and learning and a showcase for Indigenous culture around the country – is startling.

The federal government has so far remained silent on the committee's recommendations. But, as with the proposed Indigenous advisory body and the truth-telling commission, only the Commonwealth government can step up and provide the "beacon of conscience" for the entire nation and the world to see.

The philosopher Raimond Gaita recently reflected that "citizenship governed by the rule of law is a great good, but it runs deeper when nourished by love of country." As he explained, if we are to avoid jingoism, our love of country must be reflective and critical. For any of us to develop a truly honest and informed historical consciousness in Australia requires a double act: to hold both the violent dispossession of Indigenous Australians and the steady emergence of a society built on equality, democracy and freedom from racial discrimination in our imagination at the same time, and to do so by seeing from both Indigenous and non-Indigenous perspectives. A country that has the courage to look its history in the eye will be all the stronger for it.

The alternative is to hold the line of denial. Stan Grant wrote of the inevitable outcome of this: "It is as if this day – Australia Day – must pit my ancestors, white and black, in some conflict without end. It is a fight with myself I can't possibly win."

The time for pitting white against black, shame against pride, and one people's history against another's has had its day. After nearly fifty years of deeply divisive debates over the country's foundation and its legacy for Indigenous Australians, Australia stands at a crossroads – a moment of truth. We either *make* the Commonwealth stronger and more complete through an honest reckoning with the past, allowing the "ancient sovereignty" of Indigenous Australia to "shine through as a fuller expression of Australia's nationhood," or we *unmake* the nation by clinging to triumphant narratives in which the violence inherent in the nation's foundation is trivialised, and retreat once more into the old "attitudes that helped us to conquer and settle the country."

Our history will always challenge and unsettle us. To pretend otherwise is to expect a past that is predictable and lifeless – a history from which we have nothing more to learn. And there is little point in acknowledging the past only to turn away from it yet again, or else simply to condemn it as shameful. The difficulty in confronting the "complex and tragic history" to which Prime Minister Turnbull has repeatedly referred lies in accepting the fact that it has created Australia as much as Anzac, the White Australia Policy, immigration, the agendas of our governments and institutions, and the land itself. Rather than "move on" from our history, we have to bring it with us and learn how to use it to strengthen the ties that bind us as Australian citizens.

Since the early 1990s, when the Keating Labor government advanced the twin goals of reconciliation and a republic, both of which were to be achieved by the centenary of federation on 1 January 2001, Australia has been engaged in an extended project of national re-founding, the scale of which we still struggle to grasp. As with the Apology and the same-sex marriage survey, perhaps its potential will only become visible when it is achieved. We have long been on the cusp of re-founding the Commonwealth, but somehow the whole game – integrating the constitutional change embodied in the republic and reconciliation, and understanding how they speak to one another – has continued to elude us. The challenge of reconciliation is not only reconciling Aboriginal and non-Aboriginal Australians; it is also the challenge of reconciling the competing narratives of identity and nationalism that have held sway since John Howard came to power in 1996. Howard responded to Keating's dream of a republic with a more sentimental and unreflective patriotism, anchored thousands of kilometres offshore at the Gallipoli Peninsula. Keating's vision embraced a critical view of Australia's past while at the same time projecting a spirit of optimism on a large canvas, while Howard's was deeply fearful of self-examination, and preferred history that read as a "national inheritance" of honour and pride. They are two visions of Australia that have largely talked past one another, and that differ fundamentally over how Indigenous Australians should be included in the nation and represented in the constitution. Yet neither managed to truly listen to Indigenous Australians in the way that the

Uluru Statement from the Heart has since asked the Commonwealth government to do.

Perhaps now we can see one thing clearly. Our future Commonwealth will not have legitimacy or be true to the country itself if it fails to recognise unequivocally the brutality of Australia's foundation and listen to Indigenous Australians as they tell their histories in the spirit of *Makarrata* – "healing and coming together after a struggle." In the light of Australia's deep history, this is the least we can do.

*

In all of the histories from Indigenous Australians that I read while writing this essay, one image has stayed with me more than any other. It arose on Possession Island, off the northwestern tip of Cape York Peninsula, where James Cook, confident that no European had seen or visited it before him, claimed possession of the "whole eastern coast" of Australia on 22 August 1770. Coming ashore just after four o'clock in the afternoon, Cook saw a "number of people," who quickly "made off" before he led his men up to the top of a small hill, where he "hoisted the English colours," claimed possession "in the Name of His Majesty, King George the Third," gave three cheers and "fired three volleys of small Arms which were answered by the like number from the ship." From this hill, which was barely three times as high as "the Ship's Mast heads," Cook saw that he would find safe passage through the southern end of the Torres Strait.

Almost 250 years later, Gudang artist Colina Wymarra told the story as her father had passed it on to her. Cook had "put a flag on Possession Island" and, "as seafaring people," the Gudang, who often travelled there, "saw the cloth on a stick stuck in the sand on the beach," and "in their innocence" had "grabbed" it and "used it as a … covering." Wymarra painted the image of a "traditional Gudang woman as she covered herself and her baby" in the British flag. Cook made no mention of placing a flag on the beach. But of course this doesn't mean that it didn't happen. Perhaps, as they departed, one of his crew left it behind to mark their possession.

The following morning, looking through his telescope from the deck of the *Endeavour*, Joseph Banks reported seeing "3 or 4 women ... gathering shell-fish" on the same beach.

The Aboriginal people whom Cook saw as he landed on the beach would have watched him from a distance as he walked up the hill. They would have heard the voices of Cook, Banks, Daniel Solander and the rest of the party as they climbed. The sight of the *Endeavour*, anchored a mile or so offshore, its white sails rippling, would have puzzled them. But it was probably not the first time they had seen or heard of the white bird. At some point after Cook's departure, on the hill and down on the beach, they examined the traces of his presence. Footsteps. The red, white and blue cloth luminous on the sand. Taken down to wrap and warm a child.

Bound together.

SELECT BIBLIOGRAPHY

Aboriginal History (1977–present), https://press.anu.edu.au/publications/aboriginal-history-journal.

Warwick Anderson, *The Cultivation of Whiteness: Science, Health and Racial Destiny in Australia*, Melbourne University Press, 2002.

Bain Attwood, *Possession: Batman's Treaty and the Matter of History*, Melbourne University Press, 2009.

Bain Attwood, *The Good Country: The Djadja Wurrung, the Settlers and the Protectors*, Monash University Publishing, 2017.

Bain Attwood & Stephen Foster (eds), *Frontier Conflict: The Australian Experience*, National Museum of Australia, 2003.

Deborah Bird-Rose, *Hidden Histories: Black Stories from Victoria River Downs, Humbert River and Wave Hill Stations*, Aboriginal Studies Press, 1991.

Timothy Bottoms, *Conspiracy of Silence: Queensland's Frontier Killing Times*, Allen & Unwin, 2013.

James Boyce, *Van Diemen's Land*, Black Inc., 2008.

James Boyce, *1835: The Founding of Melbourne & the Conquest of Australia*, Black Inc., 2011.

Frank Brennan, *No Small Change: The Road to Recognition for Indigenous Australia*, UQP, 2015.

Richard Broome, *Aboriginal Australians: A History Since 1788*, Allen & Unwin, fourth edition, 2010.

Jane Carey & Jane Lydon (eds), *Indigenous Networks: Mobility Connections and Exchange*, Routledge, 2014.

Ian Clark, *Scars in the Landscape: A Register of Massacre Sites in Western Victoria 1803–1859*, Aboriginal Studies Press, 1995.

Nicholas Clements, *The Black War: Fear, Sex and Resistance in Tasmania*, UQP, 2014.

Coniston: The Documentary, directed by Francis Jupurrurla Kelly & David Batty, Rebel Films, 2012.

John Connor, *The Australian Frontier Wars, 1788–1838*, UNSW Press, 2002.

Libby Connors, *Warrior: A Legendary Leader's Dramatic Life and Violent Death on the Colonial Frontier*, Allen & Unwin, 2015.

Ann Curthoys & Jessie Mitchell, *Taking Liberty: Indigenous Rights and Settler Self-Government in the Australian Colonies, 1830–1890*, Cambridge University Press, 2018.

Megan Davis & George Williams, *Everything You Need to Know About the Referendum to Recognise Indigenous Australians*, New South, 2015.

Penny Edmonds, *Settler Colonialism and Reconciliation: Frontier Violence, Affective Performances and Imaginative Refoundings*, Palgrave Macmillan, 2016.

Raymond Evans, Kay Saunders & Kathryn Cronin, Exclusion, Exploitation and Extermination: Race Relations in Colonial Queensland, Sydney Australia & New Zealand Book Company, 1975.

Raymond Evans & Robert Ørsted-Jensen, "'I Cannot Say the Numbers that Were Killed': Assessing Violent Mortality on the Queensland Frontier", Social Science Research Network (online), 19 July 2017.

Final Report of the Referendum Council, Commonwealth of Australia, 30 June 2017, www.referendumcouncil.org.au/final-report.

First Australians, series of seven historical documentaries directed by Rachel Perkins, Blackfella Films, 2008.

Robert Forster & Amanda Nettleback, Out of the Silence: The History and Memory of South Australia's Frontier Wars, Wakefield Press, 2012.

Damien Freeman & Shireen Morris (eds), The Forgotten People: Liberal and Conservative Approaches to Recognising Indigenous People, Melbourne University Press, 2016.

Heather Goodall, Invasion to Embassy: Land in Aboriginal Politics in NSW 1770–1972, Allen & Unwin, 1996.

Stan Grant, The Australian Dream: Blood, History and Becoming, Quarterly Essay 64, 2016.

Anna Haebich, Broken Circles: Fragmenting Indigenous Families, 1800–2000, Fremantle Arts Centre Press, 2000.

Paul Irish, Hidden in Plain View: The Aboriginal People of Sydney, New South, 2017.

Mary Anne Jebb, Blood, Sweat and Welfare: A History of White Bosses and Aboriginal Pastoral Workers, UWA, 2002.

Miranda Johnson, The Land Is Our History: Indigeneity, Law, and the Settler State, Oxford University Press, 2016.

Benjamin Jones, This Time: Australia's Republican Past and Future, Black Inc., 2018.

Benjamin Jones & Mark McKenna, Project Republic, Black Inc., 2013.

Grace Karskens, The Colony: A History of Early Sydney, Allen & Unwin, 2009.

Shino Konishi, The Aboriginal Male in the Enlightenment World, Pickering and Chatto, London, 2012.

Shino Konishi, Maria Nugent & Tiffany Shellam (eds), Indigenous Intermediaries: New Perspectives on Exploration Archives, ANU Press, Canberra, 2015.

Zoe Laidlaw & Alan Lester (eds), Indigenous Communities and Settler Colonialism, Palgrave MacMillan, 2015.

Marcia Langton & Megan Davis, It's Our Country: Indigenous Arguments for Meaningful Constitutional Recognition and Reform, Melbourne University Press, 2016.

Darrell Lewis, A Wild History: Life and Death on the Victoria River Frontier, Monash University Publishing, 2012.

Noel Loos, *Invasion and Resistance: Aboriginal–European Relations on the North Queensland frontier, 1861–1897*, ANU Press, 1982.

Ann McGrath, *Contested Ground: Aboriginal Australians under the British Crown*, Allen & Unwin, 1995.

Russell McGregor, *Indifferent Inclusion: Aboriginal People and the Australian Nation*, Aboriginal Studies Press, 2011.

Robert Manne (ed.), *Whitewash: On Keith Windschuttle's Fabrication of Aboriginal History*, Black Inc., 2003.

Shireen Morris (ed.), *A Rightful Place: A Road Map to Recognition*, Black Inc., 2017.

A. Dirk Moses (ed.), *Genocide and Settler Society: Frontier Violence and Stolen Indigenous Children in Australian History*, Berghahn Books, 2004.

D.J. Mulvaney, *Encounters in Place: Outsiders and Aboriginal Australians, 1606–1985*, UQP, 1989.

Maria Nugent, *Botany Bay: Where Histories Meet*, Allen & Unwin, 2005.

Noel Pearson, *A Rightful Place: Race, Recognition and a More Complete Commonwealth*, Quarterly Essay 55, 2014.

Michael Powell, *Musquito: Brutality and Exile*, Fullers Bookshop, 2016.

Peter Read, *A Hundred Years War: The Wiradjuri People and the State*, ANU Press, 1988.

Peter Read & Jay Read (collectors and editors), *Long Time, Olden Time: Aboriginal Accounts of Northern Territory History*, Institute for Aboriginal Development, 1991.

Henry Reynolds, *The Other Side of the Frontier: Aboriginal Resistance to the European Invasion of Australia*, Penguin, 1981.

Henry Reynolds, *Why Weren't We Told?* Allen & Unwin, 1999.

Henry Reynolds, *Forgotten War*, New South, 2013.

Tony Roberts, *Frontier Justice: A History of the Gulf Country to 1900*, UQP, 2005.

Thomas James Rogers & Stephen Bain, "Genocide and Frontier Violence in Australia", *Journal of Genocide Research*, Vol. 18, No. 1, 2016, pp. 83–100.

Charles Rowley, *The Destruction of Aboriginal Society*, Penguin, 1972.

Tim Rowse, *Indigenous and Other Australians Since 1901*, New South, 2017.

Lynette Russell (ed.), *Colonial Frontiers: Indigenous European Encounters in Settler Societies*, Manchester University Press, 2001.

Lyndall Ryan, *Tasmanian Aborigines: A History Since 1803*, Allen & Unwin, 2012.

W.E.H. Stanner, *After the Dreaming: Black and White Australians – An Anthropologist's View*, Boyer Lectures, ABC, 1968.

Mark Tedeschi, *Murder at Myall Creek*, Simon & Schuster, 2016.

Don Watson, *Caledonia Australis: Scottish Highlanders on the Frontier of Australia*, Vintage, 2009 (first published 1984).

Patrick Wolfe, 'Settler Colonialism and the Elimination of the Native', *Journal of Genocide Research*, Vol. 8, No. 4, 2006, pp. 387–409.

SOURCES

1–2 Jimmy Clements and John Noble: Malcolm Allbrook, "Life Sentences: Neither Beaten nor Bowed", *ANU Reporter*, Vol. 49, No.1, https://reporter.anu.edu.au/life-sentences-neither-beaten-nor-bowed; Paul Daley, "Sovereignty Never Ceded: How Two Indigenous Elders Changed Canberra's Big Day', *Guardian*, 7 May 2017; Mark McKenna, *This Country: A Reconciled Republic*, UNSW Press, 2004, pp. 73–4.

2 "Aborigines ... were an insult": Fred Maynard, writing with A.E. Mckenzie-Hatton, in Bain Attwood, *The Struggle for Aboriginal Rights: A Documentary History*, Allen & Unwin, 1999, pp. 71–3; Yirrkala Petition, pp. 202–3.

2 "expropriated", "denied", etc.: The best analysis of Cooper's activism is Bain Attwood's *Rights for Aborigines*, Allen & Unwin, 2003, pp. 54–78; Cooper's letter to Lyons (written with trade unionist and fellow Christian Arthur Burdeu) can be found in Andrew Markus (ed.), *Blood from a Stone: William Cooper and the Australian Aborigines League*, Monash Publications in History No. 2, 1986, pp. 77–83.

3 "White men": Cooper's letter to Lyons, 31 March 1938 (written with trade unionist and fellow Christian Arthur Burdeu) is discussed in Bain Attwood's *Rights for Aborigines*, pp. 74–6; original in National Archives (Canberra), A659, 1940/1/858. Cooper had the idea for a Day of Mourning on Australia Day and it was discussed by Cooper, Burdeu and Bill Ferguson at a meeting in November 1937 (Attwood, pp. 69–70).

3 "horror and fear of extermination", in Attwood, *Rights for Aborigines*, p. 69; see also https://aiatsis.gov.au/exhibitions/day-mourning-26th-january-1938.

4 John Gale's story: "Mr. John Gale Enters His 100th Year", *Sydney Morning Herald*, 17 April 1929, p. 18; press reports on Kurrajong Hill, "Hundred Years of Settlement: Canberra to Celebrate", *Mercury*, 5 February 1938, p. 15; *Mercury*, 18 June 1928, p. 8.

4 "local and regional Aboriginal people": ACT Heritage, *Corroboree Ground and Aboriginal Cultural Area, Queanbeyan River*, background information, November 2017, www.environment.act.gov.au/__data/assets/pdf_file/0017/1130462/Background-Information.pdf.

4 Uncle Boydie Turner delivering Cooper's petition: "Queen Accepts Petition for Aboriginal Rights, 80 Years On", *Sydney Morning Herald*, 4 October 2014.

7 "They will do anything": Pat Anderson, quoted in Bridget Brennan, "Garma Festival: Turnbull, Shorten Criticised for 'Empty Platitudes' over Indigenous Recognition", ABC News (online), 5 August 2017.

7   "symbolic constitutional change", "can", etc.: Amanda Vanstone, "Appendix E: Qualifying Statement from Amanda Vanstone", *Final Report of the Referendum Council*, Commonwealth of Australia, 30 June 2017, pp. 65–7.

8   "Our democracy": Department of the Prime Minister and Cabinet, *Response to Referendum Council's Report on Constitutional Recognition* (media release), 26 October 2017.

9   "I don't need evidence": Dan Conifer, Bridget Brennan, Isabella Higgins, Joanna Cruthers and Shahni Wellington, "Indigenous Advisory Board Proposal Rejected by PM in 'Kick in the Guts' for Advocates", ABC News (online), 26 October 2017.

9   "What's wrong", etc.: Malcolm Turnbull and Teela Reid, *Q&A*, ABC TV, 11 December 2017.

10   "designed to give momentum": Michael Gordon, "Nation's Wound Close to Being 'Healed'", *Sydney Morning Herald*, 13 February 2013.

10   "unhealed wound", etc.: *Sydney Morning Herald*, 13 February 2013.

10   "Abbott … rushed to Facebook": Stephen Fitzpatrick, "Turnbull Broke Our Hearts", *Weekend Australian*, 28–29 October 2017, p. 10.

11   "Bipartisanship … agreement to do nothing": Calla Wahlquist, "Bill Shorten Says Labor Will Pursue Indigenous Voice to Parliament Without Coalition", *Guardian*, 12 February 2018.

11   "lived experience", "begin the detailed design work", etc.: Stephen Fitzpatrick, "PM Must Heed Uluru Call: Rudd": *Australian*, 14 February 2018.

11   "inspiring and unifying," etc.: Harry Hobbs, "Response to Referendum Council Report Suggsts a Narrow Path Forward on Indigenous Constitutional Reform", *Conversation*, 18 July 2017.

12   "Turnbull had privately expressed his support": Noel Pearson, "Prime Minister's Rejection is a Kick in the Guts for Aboriginal Australians", *Weekend Australian*, 28–29 October 2017, Inquirer, p. 24.

12   "I think you can kiss": Patricia Karvelas, "Negotiating a Way Towards Indigenous Recognition", *Weekend Australian*, 18–19 April 2015, p. 19.

12   "It's not going to deal with the Constitution": Mick Dodson, interviewed by Karen Middleton, *Saturday Paper*, 7 October 2017.

13   "a sightlessness towards Aboriginal lives": W.E.H. Stanner, "The History of Indifference Thus Begins", *Aboriginal History*, 1977, Vol. 1, No. 1, pp. 23–4.

14   "sweat blood": *Sydney Morning Herald*, 11 December 2014.

15   "The Australian people know": Galarrwuy Yunupingu, "Rom Watangu: The Law of the Land", *Monthly*, July 2016.

15   "something in the Australian psyche": Mick Dodson, "On Fixing the Constitution", *Saturday Paper*, 7 October 2017.

15–16 "Australian conscience", "there was more", etc.: Stanner, "The History of Indifference Thus Begins", pp. 23–4.

16–17 "attitudes that helped us": Judith Wright, *Because I Was Invited*, Oxford University Press, 1975 p. 185.

17 "When the massacres occurred", "shot by a man", etc.: Yunupingu, "Rom Watangu".

17 "a much more robust idea": Marcia Langton in her response to Germaine Greer's *Whitefella Jump Up*, Quarterly Essay 12, 2003, p. 78.

18 "larger culture war": Robert Manne, *In Denial: The Stolen Generations and the Right*, Quarterly Essay 1, Black Inc., 2001.

20 "in the footnotes": Bain Atwood's comments can also be found in his "The Founding of Aboriginal History and the Forming of Aboriginal History," *Aboriginal History*, Vol. 36, 2012, pp. 119–71.

24 "it was a wave": Yunupingu, "Rom Watangu".

27 "pronounced the death": Henry Reynolds, "The Breaking of the Great Australian Silence: Aborigines in Australian Historiography 1955–1983", University of London, Institute of Commonwealth Studies, Australian Studies Centre, 1984.

27 "three broad categories": Australian Bureau of Statistics, *Year Book 1968*, No. 54, ABS, 1968.

27 "just under half", etc.: George Megalogenis, "The Changing Face of Australia", *Australian Foreign Affairs*, No. 1, October 2017, p. 74.

28 "a brief but significant moment in time": Mike Smith to me, 26 January 2018.

28 "shameful", etc.: Peter Carey, in Andrew Purcell, "Peter Carey", *Sydney Morning Herald*, Spectrum, 28–29 October 2017 pp. 18–19.

29 "members on the station": Kim Scott, "The not-so-barren ranges", *Thesis Eleven*, Vol. 135, No. 1, pp. 67–81.

29 "reconciliation literature": see Jane Gleeson-White, "Properly Alive: *Taboo* by Kim Scott", *Sydney Review of Books*, 22 August 2017. Also note Chris Conti's essay, "Grenville on the Frontier", *Sydney Review of Books*, 4 May 2017.

30 "the endemic forgetfulness": Tom Griffths, *The Art of Time Travel*, Black Inc. 2016 p. 157.

30 "formed a nation": John Howard, Address at Ceremonial Sitting to Mark the Centenary of the High Court of Australia, Supreme Court of Victoria, Melbourne, 6 October 2003.

31 Citizenship booklet: *Australian Citizenship: Our Common Bond*, Commonwealth of Australia, Canberra, 2012, www.homeaffairs.gov.au/Citizenship/Documents/our-common-bond-2014.pdf, see especially pp. 12, 58, 62.

32 "What happened all across Australia": *Final Report of the Referendum Council*, 2017, p. 17.

32   "a position will have been reached": Bob Hawke's remarks in an unpublished press release, 12 June 1988, reproduced in Henry Reynolds, *Dispossession: Black Australians and White Invaders*, Allen & Unwin, 1989, pp. 213–14.

32   "nationwide emotional release", "gesture of atonement": "On Apology", *Sydney Morning Herald*, editorial, 14 February 2008.

33   Numbers of British emigrants: Quoted by Zoe Laidlaw & Alan Lester, in the opening chapter of their edited collection, *Indigenous Communities and Settler Colonialism: Land Holding, Loss and Survival in an Interconnected World*, Palgrave Macmillan, p. 5.

33   "the whole venture was premised": Henry Reynolds, *Forgotten War*, New South Press, 2013, p. 50.

33   "as Bain Attwood has shown recently": Bain Attwood, "Denial in a Settler Society: The Australian Case", *History Workshop Journal*, Oxford University Press, 2017.

34   "equitable sovereignty", "equal custodianship": Ossie Cruse to me, 17 January 2018.

34–5 "since at least the eighteenth century, if not before": Among archaeologists and historians, the question of exactly when Makassan contact with Aboriginal people began remains contested. See Marshall Clark and Sally K. May, "Understanding the Macassans: A Regional Approach", *Macassan History and Heritage*, ANU E Press, Canberra, 2013.

35–6 "the Portugese and Spanish": Archbishop John Bede Polding to Cardinal Franzoni, "Report on the Mission in Australia to 1846"; Propaganda Fide Archives, Vatican City, Rome, "Oceania", Vol. 3, leaves 16–17; translated in Stefano Girola and Rolando Pizzini (eds), *Nagoyo: The life of don Angelo Confalonieri among the Aborigines of Australia*, Fondazione Museo Storico del Trentino, 2013, pp. 39–68 at 48–51.

36   "one of the most persistent features": Henry Reynolds, *Forgotten War*, p. 50.

36–7 "We were to cut off", "a rotten spungy bog": Watkin Tench, *A Narrative of the Expedition to Botany Bay and A Complete Account of the Settlement at Port Jackson*, L.F. Fitzhardinge (ed.), Library of Australian History, Sydney, 1979, pp. 205–16.

37   Coniston Massacre: Bill Wilson and Justin O'Brien, "'To Infuse a Universal Terror': A Reappraisal of the Coniston killings", *Aboriginal History*, Vol. 27, 2003.

37   "seething with indignation", etc.: Peter Read, "Murder, Revenge and Reconciliation on the North-Eastern Frontier", *History Australia*, Vol. 4, No. 1, 2007, 09.1–09.15.

38   "only makes peoples' eyes glaze over", "The biggest argument", etc.: Lyndall Ryan to me, 9 January 2018. See also "Mapping the Massacres of Australia's Colonial Frontier", University of Newcastle website, 5 July 2017, www.newcastle.edu.au/newsroom/featured-news/mapping-the-massacres-of-australias-colonial-frontier; Ceridwen Dovey, "The Mapping of Massacres", *New Yorker*, 6 December 2017.

40–1 "Those Kartiya" and "Another crime": Jimmy Manngayarri, recalling events from the early twentieth century in *Yijarni: True Stories from Gurindji Country* (2016), an extraordinary bilingual publication, which includes the voices of many Gurindji historians from the Victoria River District in the Northern Territory, home of the 1966 Wave Hill Walk-Off. The book is the result of a collaborative project years in the making. Yijarni means "true stories." See pp. 1, 62, 65.

41–2 "They camped" and "This (Daguragu)": Ronnie Wavehill Wirrpngayarri, in *Yijarni*, recounting a massacre at Warluk (Seale Gorge), in the late nineteenth century, pp. 37–8.

42 "Further downstream": Ronnie Wavehill Wirrpngayarri (2014) in *Yijarni*, telling the story of a massacre at Waniyi (near Number 2 bore). p. 53.

42 "They got one": Emily Murray, Girramay and Jirrbal Traditional Owner, 2012; the story refers to events near Rockingham Bay in Queensland, where a guerrilla war was fought along the coast and nearby islands in the 1860s and 1870s. Recorded in the *Encounters* exhibition catalogue, National Museum of Australia, Canberra, 2015, p. 115.

43 "At another windmill": Mavis Arnott, Jigalong, 2008. Quoted by Peter Johnson and Sue Davenport, in *Ngurra Kuju Walya: One Country One People; Stories from the Canning Stock Route*, 2011, p. 338.

43 "Our history is": Donny Wooladgoodja, Dambeemangaddee people, North West Kimberley, in *Barddabardda Wodjenangorddee: We're Telling All of You; The Creation, History and People of Dambeemangaddee Country*, 2017, p. 95.

44–5 "Cook did not discover us", etc.: *Final Report of the Referendum Council*, p. 17.

47 "This statue speaks": Stan Grant, "America Tears Down Its Racist History, We Ignore Ours", ABC News (online), 20 August 2017.

47 "disgraceful": Stan Grant, quoted in Cameron Mee and James Robertson, "Vandals Deface Hyde Park Statues in Australia Day Protest", *Sydney Morning Herald*, 26 August 2017.

47 "We don't get to choose": Scott Morrison, "Why I Cherish 26 Jan in All Its Complexity", *Australian*, 4 September 2017.

48–9 Wran's nomination of Kurnell: "Kurnell Beats the Rocks to the Title Birthplace of a Nation," *The St. George and Sutherland Shire Leader*, 10 June 1981, p. 30.

49 Repainting the sign at Kurnell: "Birthplace Sign Is Right After Difficult Labor", *The St. George and Sutherland Shire Leader*, 30 October 1984.

49–50 Tracey Aubin, "White Man's Sites Are Looking More Profane than Sacred," *Sydney Morning Herald*, 29 August 1987.

50–1 "For some time": Sutherland Shire Council Mayoral Minute No. 7/93.

51 "the greatest country in the world", etc.: Malcolm Turnbull, with Neil Mitchell, 3AW (radio), 25 August 2018.

52   "the centenary of British possession": *Weekly Times* (Melbourne), 23 April 1870, p. 11.

52   "given us this country in trust": *Daily Telegraph*, 29 April 1909, p. 9.

52   "Be Patriotic": *Sydney Morning Herald*, 13 March 1915, p. 12.

52   "old hulk", "crudely painted": Commonwealth of Australia: Inaugural celebrations" 1901, "Picnic at Kurnell," pp. 195–204 (PDF obtained from Sutherland Shire Library).

53   "thousands of her dead": *Sydney Mail*, 28 April 1920, p. 10.

53   "'Mecca' for millions of tourists": *The Propeller* (Hurstville), 8 July 1937, p. 6.

53   "what Plymouth Rock is to America": *Immigration and Tourism Bureau, Kurnell Birthplace of Australian History*, 1909 (booklet).

53   "cave-dwellers", etc.: "On the Road to Kurnell", *The Propeller* (Hurstville), 8 July 1937, p. 6.

54   "the natives": Cook's remarks on the "natives" are from his journal, 23 August 1770.

55   "Koori genocide", etc.: *The St. George and Sutherland Shire Leader*, 27 April 1995, p. 1.

55   "not celebrating": *The St. George and Sutherland Shire Leader*, 2 May 1995, p. 3.

55   "a marketing effort": *The St. George and Sutherland Shire Leader*, 4 May 1999, p. 13.

55   "had agreed": Official endorsement of the Meeting of Cultures by the local Aboriginal community at Kurnell, contained in Council correspondence, 14 October 2002, EHC114-03 Minutes of the Meeting of the Kurnell Campaign, Committee of the Council of Sutherland Shire, 10 September 2002, File Number: 01/0212.

56   "blacking up": Bruce Baird & Beryl Timbery Beller, 'Meeting of Two Cultures', *The St. George and Sutherland Shire Leader*, 27 April 2000 & 2 May 2000.

57   On the Botany Bay Shield and Shayne Williams: *Encounters: Revealing Stories of Aboriginal and Torres Strait Islander Objects from the British Museum*, National Museum of Australia, Canberra, 2015, pp. 48–50.

57   "mangrove wood growing along the coast": Paul Irish, *Hidden in Plain View: The Aboriginal People of Coastal Sydney*, New South, 2017, p. 16.

57   On the contested provenance of the shield, see Maria Nugent & Gaye Sculthorpe, "A Shield Loaded with History: Encounters, Objects and Exhibitions", *Australian Historical Studies*, Vol. 49, No. 1, 2018, pp. 28–43; Nicholas Thomas, 'A Case of Identity: The Artefacts of the 1770 Kamay (Botany Bay) Encounter', *Australian Historical Studies*, Vol. 49, No. 1, 2018, pp. 4–27.

57–8 On Rodney Kelly and the shield: "Why an Indigenous Australian Wants the British Museum to Return His Ancestors' Shield", *Hyperallergic* (online), 19 June 2017; "Cambridge Refuses to Return Aboriginal Spears 'Stolen' by Cook", *Australian*, 17 June 2017.

59–60 For more details on Cooktown and reconciliation, see Mark McKenna, *From the Edge: Australia's Lost Histories*, Melbourne University Publishing, 2016. And for a fascinating look at Cook's journey along the east coast through the work of contemporary artists, see *East Coast Encounters: Re-Imagining 1770*, One Day Hill, 2014.

62   "History is his story": Warren Foster, South Coast History Day, Bega, 25 February 2017.

63   "the end of the Jukurrpa [Dreaming]": Rosie Nappurrula in Peggy Rockman Napaljarri and Lee Cataldi (translators), *Warlpiri Dreamings and Histories*, Yale University Press, 2011.

63   "end of the Jukurrpa as a worldview": Napaljarri and Cataldi (trans.).

64–5 "Our Aboriginal and Torres Strait Islander tribes": *Final Report of the Referendum Council*, p. 17.

67   "This is an Aboriginal nation": Kim Scott, quoted in Gleeson-White, "Properly Alive".

68   On healing and restorative truth: Annika Frieberg & C.K. Martin Chung (eds), *Reconciling with the Past: Resources and Obstacles in a Global Perspective*, Routledge, 2017, p. 4.

68   "wring our hands": Inga Clendinnen, *The History Question*, Quarterly Essay 23, 2006, p. 53.

71   "subvert the nation": *Australian*, editorial, 29 November 2017.

71   "as a nation": Waleed Aly, *Sydney Morning Herald*, 1 April 2016.

72   "Aboriginal and Torres Strait Islander ancesteral remains", "serve as a memorial": Advisory Committee for Indigenous Repatriation, *National Resting Place Consultation Report 2014*, Commercial and Administrative Law Branch, Attorney General's Department, Canberra, 2015.

72   "A national keeping place": Peter Yu, quoted in Paul Daley, "Restless Indigenous Remains", *Meanjin*, Vol. 73, No. 1, 2014.

73   "citizenship governed": Raimond Gaita, "Truth in the Time of Trump", *Meanjin*, 4 September 2017.

73   "It is as if this day": Stan Grant, "Australia Day in the Age of Anger", ABC News (online), 26 January 2018.

75   "number of people", "made off": Cook, *Journal*, 22 August 1770, in Ray Parkin (ed.), *H.M. Bark Endeavour*, Miegunyah Press, 2006 (first published 1997), pp. 438–40.

75   "put a flag", "as seafaring people", etc.: Colina Wymarra in *Encounters*, p. 174.

75–6 "Cook made no mention" and "3 or 4 women": Banks, Journal, 22 August 1770, in Parkin (ed.), *H.M. Bark Endeavour*, pp. 438–40.

Ely Ratner

It's tempting to caricature Hugh White. When you're mapping the contours of the China debate, who better to hold up as an exemplar of accommodation? And yet, having read his analyses closely, and having had the privilege of discussing Asia's future with him in person, I'll say again what I've said before: Hugh is right.

He's right that the United States and China are in an epochal competition for the heart and soul of the twenty-first century. He's right that Washington and the American people have yet to grapple with this reality in any meaningful way, much less respond accordingly. He's right that the United States is losing badly right now. And he's right that, if current trends continue, the result will be a whitewash in China's favour, leaving Australia with exceedingly difficult decisions about the direction of its foreign alignments and policies in a China-dominated Asia.

But this is where Hugh and I diverge, because I just don't think the contest is over. Nor is China's victory as inevitable as Hugh portrays. With a smart, focused strategy, the United States can staunch Beijing's momentum towards a China-led order in the region – and it can do so in ways that don't do violence to the US–Australia alliance or Australia's foreign-policy fundamentals.

If Hugh and I are fellow travellers in our depictions of current trends in Asia, what accounts for our starkly differing conclusions about where this all ends up? I see three core issues upon which Hugh and I disagree.

First, Hugh describes the purpose of the Obama administration's Pivot, or Rebalance, to Asia as an attempt to "deter Beijing from challenging US leadership by affirming America's determination to remain Asia's primary power." Later, he describes Obama's policy as a failed effort to "resist and contain China's challenge." Here, I have to say, Hugh is wrong. Having spent countless hours in the White House Situation Room in National Security Council meetings with President Obama and his national security team, I can safely say that the Obama administration's Asia policy was not focused on containing China's rise or deterring a challenge to US leadership. Geopolitical competition in Asia was not a central focus. Instead, US policy was based on the notion that China's expanding power and influence were natural, manageable and, on balance, beneficial to enhancing cooperation on global issues. (I'll admit the messaging wasn't great – another thing on which Hugh and I agree.)

This matters a great deal because it determines whether the story of the last decade is that the United States intended, attempted, but ultimately failed to resist China's rise; or, alternatively, that the United States hasn't actually tried in any meaningful way yet to apply significant counterpressure on Beijing's burgeoning influence. Hugh argues the former, I'd argue the latter. He thinks the gig is up; I think we haven't tested the proposition.

I also take issue with Hugh's characterisation that "disappointment" with Australia's approach to China was a critical factor shaping Washington's attitude towards Canberra. This is a significant misreading insofar as China was a distant priority in the Obama administration's Australia policy – certainly compared to the importance of working with Canberra on climate change, refugees and counter-ISIS campaigns in Syria and Iraq. Bottom line: Hugh overstates Washington's focus on resisting the China challenge, which leads him to see decisive failure where I still see latent potential.

Second, and relatedly, Hugh bases much of his argument on what he perceives to be an imbalance of resolve: China cares more, is more willing to go to war, and will therefore prevail in any game of chicken or brinksmanship. I agree with Hugh that Washington has been unduly risk-averse, thereby creating a permissive environment for Chinese assertiveness. But that can surely change; the United States could take a firmer line in defending its interests in Asia. In fact, I think this is more likely than not.

What would happen then? In Hugh's telling, China will stand firm and Washington will blink. Good as a theory, but also inaccurate as a depiction of recent events. It's true that Washington has exhibited significant risk aversion – but so has Beijing. Look at the record: in instances where the Obama (and now Trump) administration outlined clear and credible consequences for China's bad behaviour – including on cyber-espionage, UN sanctions on North Korea, and its Air Defense Identification Zone in the East China Sea – Beijing quickly folded and reversed course. In fact, it's hard to think of a single case where China escalated in the face of concentrated, principled American power. Contrary to Hugh's predictions, this suggests that when the United States chooses to push back, Beijing isn't quite so willing after all to lower its shoulder at the risk of confrontation.

Third, Hugh ascribes limited and minimal aims to China's leaders, noting that "they will seek no more influence in East Asia, and over Australia, than they need to achieve their key objectives." This sounds fairly benign, and it is a point often made by those in Washington who argue that US policy in Asia is basically on the right course. I'm less confident, and further troubled by descriptions of geo-politics in Asia suggesting that all that's really happening is one balloon is getting bigger and one balloon is getting smaller. For me, this kind of normative relativism – or at least normative agnosticism – elides just how different China's control of Asia could be. It's worth thinking critically about an illiberal world in which the Chinese Communist Party has dominant sway over the norms, rules and institutions that govern international relations. Admittedly, neither politicians nor experts in Washington have made this case clearly or effectively, but that doesn't mean the consequences will be small and acceptable if Beijing consolidates a China-led order. I see sky-high stakes for the United States.

In the final analysis, Hugh's essay is exceedingly important as a clarion call – I wish every senior US policy-maker would take the time not only to read it, but to internalise the profundity of the challenge facing the United States. That said, the United States is not as weak nor is China as strong as Hugh's readers might be led to believe. To friends in Australia, let me conclude with this: America is down but not out. Stick with us. Ride out Donald Trump. Our alliance can still help preserve a future for Asia that is open and free. It's not yet time, as Hugh suggests, to submit to a region without America.

Ely Ratner

Correspondence

Michael Green & Evan S. Medeiros

Hugh White's essay demonstrates that even a flawed argument can garner international attention if it uses the right dramatic device. For White, that device is a fictional meeting of the US National Security Council (NSC). In this vignette, the President chooses not to risk war, potentially nuclear war, with China over the South China Sea; in doing so, according to White, the United States effectively retreats from Asia and hands it to China. This is exciting stuff indeed and we look forward to the movie.

However, the reality of national security policy-making is seldom so dramatic and simplistic. We have heard the binary "China Choice" argument for nearly a decade now, but this particular vignette and newest version of White's argument caught our attention not only due to its colour and flair but also its factual inaccuracy and analytic weakness. Given our collective participation in over a decade of actual meetings on China in the White House Situation Room for Presidents Bush and Obama, we have a very different view about this fictional NSC meeting, as well as the broader geopolitical dynamics at play in the Asia-Pacific.

White's argument is built on a rolling series of inflated assumptions about Chinese power, and deflated assumptions about the United States. His argument also displays the core analytic flaw of generalisation: it assumes the specific case of the South China Sea is the best and only way to measure US resolve more broadly (and that US resolve is best tested by a willingness to escalate to nuclear war with China). White also selectively interprets the events in the South China Sea to make the case for a US retreat from Asia, which we see as an overly sweeping conclusion. In addition, there is almost no extended discussion of economic issues, as if economic interdependence is irrelevant to Asian nations' strategic orientation. (White just asserts widespread economic *dependence* on China by everyone in Asia.)

To be clear, we do not question White's motives in trying to foster a serious debate about the implications of China's growing clout and ambition; indeed we applaud his efforts. We do, however, question his analytic judgments about the capabilities, motives, possible scenarios and likely outcomes. Such a debate needs to be well informed and well reasoned. We would like to see less polemics and more analytics.

Let us begin with China. White's ledger sheet on China's power lists only profits and potential profits – no losses or potential losses. He does a great job of measuring China's strengths and juxtaposing them against America's weaknesses. Neither of us has any illusions about China's economic, diplomatic or military capabilities and potential; Xi Jinping is clearly a formidable leader with substantial ambitions. However, China's limitations and weaknesses are substantial as well: an economy saddled with a large and growing debt burden, a bloated and inefficient state sector, endemic corruption, a highly inefficient system for allocating resources, pervasive and extreme air and water pollution, and a leadership that is, at best, ambivalent about market reforms. China desperately wants to avoid the middle-income trap but, if history is a guide, it only has only about five years left before demographic trends and related macro-economic imbalances become structural constraints to doing so.

Externally, China's dependence on foreign energy sources is only growing, creating major vulnerabilities. Its military capabilities are untested in conflict, and few of China's top military leaders have any real combat experience aside from a costly ground campaign with Vietnam in 1979. Diplomatically, China enjoys very little attractive soft power, and its coercive use of its economic, military and paramilitary capabilities in recent years has fostered enduring anxiety in Asia. The US Pivot was premised on the correct assumption that no one in Asia wants China to dominate the region, and that remains the case today – perhaps more so as Xi Jinping shows his stripes.

In contrast, White's ledger sheet on the United States is presented as all losses or projected losses. There is no mention of American energy dominance; the United States' broad and increasingly strong economic recovery (projected to continue, absent an exogenous shock); the strengthening of American alliances in Asia, America's technological innovation, higher education institutions, military capabilities; or the fact that direct foreign investment into the United States from Asian sources dwarfs that going into China in both stock and flow.

More to the point, White's essay assumes that the United States is incapable of learning and adjusting to the new reality, whereas China is capable of flawlessly mastering every strategic twist and turn, and incapable of error or overreach. For example, he argues that many American policy-makers and experts think the best way to deal with China is to wait for it to collapse politically, economically and diplomatically, and that US policy has been based on such assumptions. White should name one such policy-maker, because we are not aware of anyone on either side of the aisle who has made that argument. Such arguments certainly never came up in the NSC meetings we have attended since 2001. This is a classic straw-man argument about US policy.

On the same theme of blissful American complacency, Hugh argues that China's coercive actions on maritime issues have worked well for Beijing because Washington has made no effective response; he then concludes that China has won by default. We have each noted, as have many of our American colleagues in and out of government, that Beijing gained a strategic advantage in its rapid and unexpected construction and partial militarisation of island bases in the South China Sea. The United States, Australia and our partners then suffered further setbacks when Beijing was able to use proxies within both ASEAN and the European Union to block consensus in those groupings and blunt diplomatic pressure on China. A goal scored for China perhaps, but White would have us throw in the towel and go back to the bus for a depressing ride home in the first minutes of the game.

White's accounts of Chinese behaviour in the East and South China Seas are inaccurate in their characterisation of the events and their outcomes (that is, China always winning). He claims that China's moves against Scarborough Shoal and the Senkaku Islands were deliberate and carefully planned and executed attempts to test US resolve – and that the US failed in both instances. His account does not accord with the facts.

In May 2012, the dispute over Scarborough Shoal near the Philippines came about because a Philippine naval vessel (on the way back from monitoring a North Korean missile test) stumbled by chance upon a Chinese fisherman fishing within the shoal. The navy arrested the fisherman and thus began the dispute with China. Beijing and Manila spent several *weeks* trying to resolve this privately – which Beijing clearly preferred. The situation escalated when the Philippines unwisely went public and sought to shame China into cooperating. China then escalated further by deploying coastguard vessels in and around the disputed shoal. Keep in mind that China's position on the South China Sea at that time was heavily influenced by Hu Jintao and State Councillor Dai Bingguo, who were both known to prefer diplomacy and were still committed to a low-profile foreign policy ("hide and bide"). Thus, the notion that the 2012 Scarborough Shoal incident was a grand strategic play by Hu Jintao is a bit rich. To be sure, China outmanoeuvred Washington and Manila, albeit mendaciously, by keeping its vessels around Scarborough and thus securing de facto control of the area, but this lesson was not lost on other countries in the region.

That is not the end of the story. China threatened many times to take similar action in and around another disputed feature, Thomas Shoal (where a very old, rusting Philippine naval vessel is grounded), but never made a move to do so. The US and Philippine militaries worked together to keep the naval vessel and its occupants well supplied, and deterred Chinese efforts to seize the shoal.

Even more dramatically, in 2016 the United States very specifically deterred China from conducting land reclamation in Scarborough Shoal. According to press reports, in early March 2016 US intelligence agencies gained information that China was preparing to send dredgers to Scarborough to begin reclamation; by some accounts, a few ships had already left Chinese ports. With this information, and after a few NSC meetings (okay, sometimes these meetings can involve drama), Washington decided to intervene at the highest levels. During a 31 March meeting with Xi Jinping at the Nuclear Security Summit, President Obama made clear that if China started reclamation work at Scarborough it would have major consequences, implying US military action; he linked this to the credibility of US alliance commitments. Xi Jinping clearly got the message, because Chinese ships turned around and the Scarborough reclamation was halted. In other words, China backed down.

A similar course of events played out in the East China Sea. In this case, Chinese actions were not a well-planned effort to test US and Japanese resolve, but a gradual evolution of events precipitated by Japanese actions. China deployed its coastguard around the disputed islands because the islands had been effectively nationalised by the Japanese government. Tokyo thought it had successfully managed this issue with Beijing between the announcement in July and its implementation in September, but once the decision took effect, Beijing reacted with anger and numerous deployments.

The US and Japanese response was not the unmitigated failure that White purports it to be in his essay. On the contrary, from autumn 2012, the United States and Japan countered Chinese coercion in the East China Sea. US diplomacy, military deployments and coordination with Japan prevented China from escalating its presence around the disputed islands, after multiple Chinese attempts to do so. Washington and Tokyo outflanked Xi diplomatically in the region and prevented him from demonising Prime Minister Abe and isolating Japan. Tokyo stepped up Japanese capabilities around the Senkakus, and Chinese actions produced the dramatic revision of the US–Japan defence cooperation guidelines. Far from "winning," Xi abandoned his original conditions for concessions on the Senkakus and agreed to a summit with Abe in November 2014.

This evolution of US commitment towards Asia continues under the Trump administration. We have each criticised this president from opposite sides of the aisle for abandoning the Trans-Pacific Partnership, hobbling the State Department, questioning US alliances and damaging America's brand in many parts of the world. There are strategic consequences to these actions, to be sure. But the Trump administration has also made the response to China a central organising tenet of its new National Security Strategy, imperfect though that strategy may still be. Secretary of Defense James Mattis has made more trips to meet with friends and allies in Asia than any of his predecessors in their first year, and has accelerated the Pentagon's rebalance to Asia, despite Trump's ridiculous campaign pledges threatening to abandon allies who did not pay more for their defence (though we would be quick to add that allies, including Australia, *should* spend more on defence).

Moreover, while Trump's statements and actions (and the frequent disconnect between them) make for an irresistible target for White, polls show that support among the American public for global engagement and free trade actually *increased* in 2017. Indeed, a majority of Americans now identify Asia as the most important region in the world to our nation's future. That percentage skyrockets among millennials. This is equally true for the Congress, where internationalists are winning seats in both parties and a growing cadre of new members is making Asia, rather than Europe or the Middle East, the focus of their legislative careers.

White's fantastical scenario of an Asia without America ignores all of this. It also ignores two centuries of American engagement in the region. The American foreign policy intellectual Walter Lippman argued just before World War II that American isolationism applied to Europe, but never really applied to the Pacific. After France fell in 1940, Gallup polls showed that Americans still wanted to sit out the war in Europe, but were willing to put more pressure on Japan to back off in the Pacific, "even at the risk of war." The United States bled in the Pacific during the Cold War, not in Europe. White argues that Americans will not be willing to risk nuclear war to defend allies in Asia, but the American people and Congress were willing to do so to defend NATO and Japan during the Cold War, and polls today show the highest level of public support for the defence of Japan or Korea, if needed, than we have ever seen. The "tripwire" that will guarantee American deterrence in Asia is not just American bases, but the hundreds of thousands of Americans who live in the region. The American territory of Guam is closer to mainland China than any point in Australia.

White's essay is also ahistorical in arguing that the correct metric of American power is the retention of primacy in Asia. Even if one posits a more precipitous shift in power in the region – and there are many reasons not to believe we are on the eve of a shift to Chinese primacy as White claims – the reality is that since 1783 American leaders have focused first and foremost on preventing rival hegemons from denying the United States access to the Pacific. After 1945, primacy was, for a time, arguably a means to that end – not a historic end in itself. When Nixon opened to China in 1971 to counterbalance Soviet hegemony after Vietnam, he was acting in the tradition of Theodore Roosevelt, who had understood how to play a multipolar power dynamic to maintain American access and advantage. The conditions for this strategy are no less ripe in Asia today. With the exception of Russia, the most powerful states in the region are moving closer to the United States because of uncertainty about China.

Furthermore, according to Hugh White, the fundamental test of primacy (as bad a metric as it may be) is not just US willingness to go to war with China over the South China Sea, but willingness to engage in nuclear war. Such a standard for measuring US resolve says more about White's anxieties about the United States than the strategic realities of the Asia-Pacific. As former staff of the National Security Council, we are confident in asserting that it is essentially unknowable what the conditions might be for the United States to escalate to nuclear war with China, over the South China Sea, Taiwan or any issue. The specific evolution of such a crisis matters enormously. In our collective eleven years of service on the NSC staff, and after countless hours of meetings with allies and partners alike, we were never asked if the United States was willing to escalate to nuclear war with China as a signal of US resolve to back its security commitments in Asia. Not to put too fine a point on it, but this is a phony test.

White's dismissal of the other powers in Asia is perhaps the flimsiest assumption of all. In his imagined post-American world, India would have insufficient reach into the Pacific, and Japan would be too isolated within East Asia to lead without America – ipso facto, the other major powers are irrelevant to this contest, now and in the future. But wait a minute: what if we look at the real world we know about first, instead of the post-American world Hugh posits? The fact that Japan, Australia and India all quickly agreed to participate in a "Quad" strategic dialogue with the United States that each had avoided earlier demonstrates an important shift in those countries' strategic preferences for balancing Chinese power. The defence, intelligence and diplomatic relationships the United States has with Japan, India and Australia are unprecedented and slated to grow further. In terms of strategic alignment, we agree that China has had success wooing or intimidating some Southeast Asian countries. Beijing might also think it is winning in Korea under President Moon Jae-in, though polls there show deepening mistrust of China and strong support for the US alliance. Meanwhile, the most successful and powerful states in the region are aligning more closely with the United States, as we noted. That dynamic, as much as any, is what precludes the post-American world that Hugh posits.

In our view, Asia is emerging as a very dynamic multipolar security system in which major powers will bob and weave for influence across the arenas of economic, diplomatic and military affairs, cooperating in some and competing in others. No one in Asia wants China to dominate, but all want to benefit from China's economy; conversely, no one in Asia wants to choose between the United States and China, but most are happy to play them off against each other. The strategic dynamics in Asia in the coming decades will be the space between these realities.

We are neither complacent about the challenges posed by China's rise and its assertions in Asia, nor are we panicked about what it means for the United States' relative position in the region – and regional politics more broadly. Australians shouldn't be either. To be sure, the United States has much to do to improve its position, but that has always been the case (regardless of the China challenge), given the substantial US economic and security interests in the region. The core functions of US alliances – reassurance, deterrence and restraint – are a full-time job in the era of North Korean nuclear weapons and the myriad transitional challenges to Asian stability. Thus, the demand for the United States in Asia remains robust and in ways and on issues that China simply lacks the capabilities and expertise to provide.

Therefore, we believe it is highly premature for Australia or any country in Asia to jump into a post-American world based on the narrative of a binary choice built on an inflated assumption of China's capabilities and deflated assumptions about US capabilities and resolve. Accordingly, we do not think that the current government of Australia is remotely close to accepting such arguments. If the latest foreign policy white paper is an accurate indication of Canberra's strategic orientation, Australian policy-makers are as clear-eyed and determined as we are about the need to address the challenges emanating from China and Xi Jinping, which means securing opportunities and cooperation with Beijing where possible. As this picture takes shape, both the United States and Australia need to have public debates about these issues, and we applaud Hugh White's effort to provoke such debate. These debates, however, need to be as well informed as they are engaging and entertaining; it is on that front which we believe White's essay could have done better.

Michael Green & Evan S. Medeiros

Patrick Lawrence

What a level, clear-eyed assessment Hugh White has written as China emerges, the United States dithers in clouds of nostalgia, and Australians must determine how to proceed amid these momentous transformations. I privilege this as my opening remark on White's intricately reasoned essay because, as an American watching Washington closely as a matter of my profession, "level" and "clear-eyed" are not terms I am accustomed to typing. White comes out right: here is what the twenty-first century looks like; take it, because there is no leaving it. "Let's get on with it," as his last sentence puts the point.

In truth, I did not begin White's piece so approvingly. I expected to read another connoisseur of the exquisite circularity of Western-centric strategic reasoning, if this is the word. The early signals were many: "America will lose, and China will win," "how the contest will proceed," "a new, China-led order," "an Asia dominated by China," "a country's willingness to go to war … determines its place in the international system," and so on. This is the zero-sum myopia that afflicts Washington: what China gains is our loss. It is an adjunct of the "indispensable nation" routine – which, in turn, gives rise to the with-us-or-against-us bit. George W. Bush made this explicit after the September 11 tragedies; but, as White reminds us, Barack Obama treated Australia to a full-dress rendering when he addressed parliament a decade and two months later.

America has the frame wrong, as White notes with a splendid bluntness. This seems to be a realisation that arrives bitterly among Australians, and one understands: it rather cancels many decades of assumptions. White walks through and out of these – the virtue of his piece. China's rise does not imply a contest. In that speech Obama delivered in Canberra in November 2011, he announced that the United States had decided to turn it into one – a very different thing. This is the frame, and it has proven the fatal flaw in American thinking ever since.

The emergence of China as a regional and global power is neither more nor less than history's wheel turning. It is a challenge, certainly – no surprise, as history is never short of these – but it is not a challenge to confront, or to turn back. That is sheer folly, as White remarks in so many words. The challenge is to find opportunities in the soil of an unfamiliar landscape. It is to advance imaginatively into a new time, confident of one's competence to do so. It is to remain game, in a word: aware of the past but never its prisoner.

White writes quite a lot about "great-power politics," hegemony, the ambitions of powerful nations. He refers severally to the nineteenth-century conduct of the European powers. Good enough to have a sound grounding in history, something we Americans flatly decline to cultivate.

But I urge White to dilate the lens still further. Parity between West and non-West, in one or another manifestation, is in my view the twenty-first century's single most momentous imperative. Humanity has known nothing like this for at least half a millennium (taking my date from da Gama's 1498 arrival in Calicut). The past is not going to be so reliable a guide, precedent not so strict a professor – this for the simple reason that non-Western nations are going to do things differently. Empire-building, to make the most obvious of many distinctions, will not figure among their priorities.

How does a nation's intent come to be as it is? Or its ambitions? What gives rise to them, and why? History, culture, traditions, long-embedded values – these, the soil of politics, are my answers. If we think about China in this way, what might we surmise?

Anyone who has walked to and fro on the mainland understands that the Opium Wars were the day before yesterday to the Chinese sensibility. So there is the question of humiliation and its overcoming – redress. The Western powers walked all over the Chinese by way of territorial integrity, but let us not stop there: pile a set of historical maps atop one another and leaf through them – what makes China China has been a question requiring careful management as long as there has been a China. Closer to our time, it is worth considering the Five Principles of Peaceful Co-Existence Zhou Enlai articulated at Bandung in 1955, when the People's Republic was a struggling six-year-old. Four had to do with mutual respect – territorial integrity, non-interference, recognition of equality, and so on.

The Cold War being as it was, China's record in these regards is other than spotless. But vastly on the whole, it indicates that Zhou, fifty-seven when he went to Bandung, was not a mere spouter of platitudes. There is a thread of continuity in China's conduct, then to now. It dropped no bombs last year and sent no drones into civilian populations in other nations. It has no record of foment-ing coups, fixing elections, or, as White points out, insisting that others adhere to its political and social ideologies.

I read Xi Jinping's monumentally sweeping speech at the Nineteenth Party Congress last October against this background. It is clear to me that China sees its best interests – stability (another long preoccupation in Beijing) and prosper-ity for its 1.3 billion people – as lying in the cultivation of these very things as far as it can go from Shanghai to Lisbon. The American dailies groused endlessly about self-interest when Xi celebrated his Belt and Road Initiative at a quite well-attended forum in Beijing last spring. This is what I mean by the opportunities that are there to be exploited but overlooked when the frame is threat and rivalry. I read the list of the 1700 BRI projects already on the books and thought, "With enemies like this, who needs friends?"

One of the decisive passages in White's piece comes after he ticks off all the worst outcomes now laid out in situation rooms in Canberra (and of course Washington). "Beijing could one day try to impose its brand of authoritarian politics, dictate national policies and control our economy to its advantage," he writes. "At worst it could invade the country and subject it to direct rule from Beijing." I had not thought our American brand of paranoia had spread so far. But then:

> There is no evidence that this is how China's leaders see things today. Their territorial ambitions seem limited to the lands that China already occupies or claims ... They show no desire to pros-elytise an ideology or export a political system. Nor do they want radical change in the regional or global economic order.

My first thought on reading this was that White would have a tough time finding a professorship in the US if he insists on tossing this kind of thing around, but that is another conversation. This is the kind of clear sight Australia needs to rely upon – a starting point, no more – as it decides how to locate itself as a Pacific nation in the twenty-first century. As to the rivalry theme, I propose to dispose of it this way: America has a lot of frontage on the Pacific lake, and no one wishes it were otherwise – not even the Chinese. They are not saying, "Go, your time is over." They are saying only, "Move over." But as White points out, the Amer-ican diplomatic tradition is far too underdeveloped – we have no gift for it because sheer power has left us with no need of it – to manage even this easily achievable subtlety.

White protests repeatedly against the common theme in Australia of recent years, "We don't have to choose." I agree it is wrong, a weak-minded flinch, but I do not agree on the choice as White describes it. Australia does have a choice to make, but it does not lie between Beijing and Washington in some contrived either/or fashion. Tipping towards paradox, Australia has to decide if it accepts the choice the US presents it with: us or them, Aussies, choose. I urge Australians to recognise this as a monumentally inconsiderate proposition on America's part, one in which Australia would do well to detect a fundamental indifference to its own interests at the core of American policy. The latter has long begun and ended with the preservation of primacy, all else judged as serving it or not. This, along with the nostalgic folly of American strategy in the Pacific, ought to make Australia's true choice a lot easier, I would think. It is the choice of refusing the choice. The truly consequential choice is America's: it lies between past and future.

I conclude with two final remarks: one has to do with global order and the other with the independence of nations within, broadly speaking, the Western alliance.

White refers often to the post-1945 order, or "the region's 'rules-based order' – by which they [the optimists in Canberra] mean the US-led status quo," as something many Australians consider the grail to be preserved as they consider their future. Fair enough. Many people in many places think this way. But I think nations such as Australia would do well to reconsider the record, as this, too, would make their deliberations easier. There are too many truisms and gloss-overs inscribed in the orthodoxy on this point. There has been an awful lot of disorder in the Western Pacific in the decades of American primacy (and indeed long before, if we go back to the war in the Philippines). It is off the point, but I must respectfully take issue with White's remark that Latin America, with its decades of dictators, civil wars, endemic poverty and violence, has by and large done well under American dominance. We – all of us, with more voices at the table and less hegemonic ambition – can do better by way of a global order worthy of the term.

"Australia is going to have a more independent foreign policy in the new Asia – more independent of Washington, that is – whether it likes it or not." So White writes midway in his essay. I do not quite comprehend the whiff of stage fright. One has long understood Australia's place as Washington's "most obliging ally," as White puts it. But for me, at least, there has always been an assumption of some ... what? ... some faint ignominy attaching to this position. Taking possession of a voice of its own will certainly bring Australia challenges and responsibilities. But how salutary a prospect nonetheless. Taking the point further, I would say even the challenges and responsibilities will do the nation a power of good.

I have wondered for decades when in hell the Europeans will learn to stand up and speak for themselves instead of dutifully yes-ing Washington even when it is diametrically against their interests to do so. They have their own perspectives, their own view of diplomacy as against conflict, much that is evolved in their address of the non-Western Other. They mutter of these things among themselves but then resume the forced march. The world would be better for this balancing voice to articulate clearly, especially as it would come from within the old Atlantic alliance.

The Europeans will soon face a series of important decisions. Do they conduct themselves as part of the Eurasian landmass as this draws together in one of the truly historic motions of our time, or stay loyal to the alliance in a way wholly lacking in imagination and confidence? White's very thoughtful essay moves me to suggest that on its side of the world – different topography, a sea and not a landmass – Australia faces a version of the very same question.

One of the truths I learnt when reporting on Indonesia during the first post-Suharto years, when various provinces were fighting for autonomy, was that to stay together it would be necessary for the Republic of Indonesia to come partially apart. Reading Hugh White's essay, I wonder if the same may now prove so of the West and all who identify as belonging to it.

Patrick Lawrence

David Shambaugh

If Hugh White's previous Quarterly Essay, *Power Shift*, and his book *The China Choice* were not controversial enough, *Without America* takes his provocative analyses of the US–China dynamic in Asia and for Australia to a new level. His previous proposal called for the United States and China essentially to form a "G2" condominium of shared hegemony over Asia. This naively ignored the deep competitive and semi-adversarial dynamics and distrust in the US–China relationship, to say nothing of the fact that no other Asian state desired such a power duopoly. What we have witnessed since these earlier publications has been a sharp intensification of the competitive dynamics, not US–China cooperation. Yet that is not the way Hugh see things.

In the latest iteration Hugh has made his arguments and analysis even more stark and extreme. *Without America* puts forward even more provocative arguments about the decline of the United States in Asia, the dominance of China, and the implications of this power shift for Australia and other states in the region. But I find his arguments to be based on a large number of fallacious assumptions, many hyperbolic and false assertions, stretched logic, and analysis devoid of evidence. The case he makes is overly stark and empirically false about both the United States *and* China's role in Asia. He way oversells China and way undersells America. He appreciates neither American resolve nor China's many vulnerabilities. As a result, he paints a false picture of Chinese dominance and American retreat. It is not only false analysis – it's dangerous, because he recommends very mistaken policies for Australia (and other regional states).

It is indeed a good thing for scholars to stir the pot and push their colleagues and the public alike to think afresh. This is one test of a public intellectual – and Hugh passes with flying colours! Routinised "groupthink" is a recipe for being caught unprepared. We must collectively thank Hugh for taking his public intellectual duty seriously and calling it as he sees it on such a critical subject. I also must say at the outset of this rejoinder that Hugh and I share a strong personal and professional relationship, which transcends our different perspectives. We have debated in the past, are debating at present, and no doubt will debate into the future. This intellectual interaction has been mutually beneficial. We agree on some things, but by no means all. My critique of his latest essay is organised around several core themes and illustrative quotations.

America's Decline and Retreat

Perhaps the most central – and controversial – of Hugh's assertions concerns the decline, retreat and withdrawal of US power and influence across the region. He writes that, "The probability therefore grows that America will peacefully, and perhaps even willingly, withdraw" and that, "under President Trump, the retreat from Asia which began under Obama is probably becoming irreversible."

This is a familiar refrain one has repeatedly heard since the Korean and Vietnam wars – yet America's regional staying power has been steadfast. Since the end of the Cold War, the United States has probably never been *more* deeply involved in, engaged with and deployed across the vast Indo-Asia-Pacific region than at present. Any number of economic, diplomatic, military and cultural indicators illustrate the breadth and depth of the American footprint. US relations with Japan and India have never been stronger, and the US–South Korea alliance remains very solid (in the face of North Korean provocations). US ties across the ten ASEAN states are uneven but sturdy. The Thai and Philippines alliances have shown signs of strain recently, but they are hardly about to disintegrate. Hugh may not think so, but US–Australia relations remain extensive and robust. Even with China, it is not a dysfunctional relationship: over US$600 billion in trade; more than 350,000 Chinese students in US universities, millions of tourists flowing in each direction; and extensive government-to-government exchanges tie the two societies together. In short, the United States is not drawing down or pulling out– it is ramping up its presence across Asia.

The Failure of the Obama Pivot?

Hugh comes to his conclusion about a retreating America from what he considers to have been a complete "failure" of the Obama Pivot policy. He says that, "The Pivot failed because there was almost nothing more to it than this declaration of intent. No substantial commitment of resources backed it up ... The architects of the Pivot in the Obama administration, and indeed the bulk of the US foreign-policy establishment, did not take China's challenge seriously." He concludes that "America's allies and friends in Asia had lost confidence in its leadership as a result."

He also contends that the Trans-Pacific Partnership "never made much sense, either economically or strategically."

I will acknowledge that Asians expected more from the Pivot, and that there was disappointment in several countries about both the rollout and the implementation. But to dismiss it as a complete failure and to assert that there was nothing substantive to it ignores the following facts:

- There was sustained high-level diplomatic engagement of *all* Indo-Asian countries. President Obama himself visited every single East Asian state except Brunei. This was also true of the secretary of state and other senior cabinet officials. Twelve Asian heads of state were received at the White House.
- The US–India relationship was taken to an all-time high, Myanmar was lifted out of isolation, Vietnam and the United States built a solid foundation for future ties (including lifting the arms embargo), while Singapore solidified its already close strategic partnership.
- The five US alliances were all strengthened – before the 2014 coup in Thailand and President Duterte's election in the Philippines.
- Defence cooperation across the region was significantly enhanced through agreements with the Philippines, Singapore and India. Similar upgrading of military cooperation with Australia, Japan, Malaysia, South Korea and Vietnam occurred.
- The US defence footprint across the Indo-Pacific *increased* significantly under the Pivot to include approximately 325,000 military and civilian personnel in the US Pacific Command theatre. The US Pacific Fleet alone includes six aircraft carrier battle groups, approximately 180 ships and submarines, 1500 aircraft, and 100,000 personnel. US forces are forward deployed in Hawaii, Guam, the Marianna Islands, Japan, South Korea, Australia and Kyrgyzstan – and they rotate regularly through Thailand, Malaysia, Singapore, Brunei and the Philippines. Similar arrangements are under discussion with India. Under the Pivot the US committed to maintaining 60 per cent of its naval assets in Asia. This is hardly a drawdown in military power, as White asserts.
- The Trans-Pacific Partnership was successfully negotiated – which showed American regional economic leadership until President Trump mistakenly withdrew.
- US public diplomacy also increased significantly, including the very successful Young Southeast Asian Leaders Initiative.

These are certainly not indicators of a "failed" policy or a declining power. In fact, with the exception of US–China and US–North Korea relations, American ties with every single country across the Indo-Pacific *improved* on Obama's watch. He was truly America's first "Pacific President." So I don't know what Hugh is talking about when he argues that America is withdrawing from Asia, or that the Pivot was a failure.

China Dominates Asia?

Also central to Hugh's arguments are his claims that China is dominating Asia and Washington is doing nothing to resist it. He writes that, "Under Trump, America seems to have abandoned the objective of resisting China's challenge in Asia ... The administration has scarcely acknowledged that America faces a strategic contest with China in Asia." He goes further to assert:

> The most likely outcome is now becoming clear. America will lose, and China will win. America will cease to play a major strategic role in Asia, and China will take its place as the dominant power ... Now it is China that is facing down America ... To preserve its leadership, America must convince China that it is willing to go to war to resist China's challenge ... The Chinese seem convinced that America will surrender regional leadership rather than risk a war with China ... Beijing has been deliberately creating situations in some of these flashpoints to test America's resolve ... Washington has made no effective response, and that has allowed China to win by default ... The only escape is to hope China backs off.

Finally, Hugh claims that "there is still a lot of wishful thinking in Washington about China. Too many people there think that the best course is to wait for it to collapse, economically, politically, and diplomatically" and, "The biggest mistake US policy-makers have made in dealing with China has been to underestimate how determined it is to replace America as East Asia's leading power."

This is all nonsense. I live and work in Washington, I interact with American officials and strategists all the time, and it is fair to say that there is no single strategic issue that more preoccupies them than China. This was true under Obama and it remains true under Trump. The recent National Security Strategy of the United States (somewhat similar to Australia's foreign policy white paper) is extremely clear about the priority of resisting a range of threats from China. Released after Hugh's essay, this important document is clear counterevidence to his assertions. Figuring out how to counter China is big business in Washington, and there now exists a sober consensus across the spectrum of strategists that the old tools of "engagement" are no longer applicable to countering a broad range of Chinese challenges to American interests. And Hugh's bizarre assertion that Washington is blindly waiting for China to collapse is sheer fiction. That is by no means an operative assumption, including by myself.

On the Chinese side of the equation, I searched in vain throughout Hugh's essay for any empirical evidence for his "China-dominating-Asia" thesis. Only on page 33 does he state: "And of course China has a lot to offer [Asia]." Then he cites the Asian Infrastructure Investment Bank and the Belt and Road Initiative. He could have provided some statistics on trade and investment, which are the heart of China's regional power. And *how exactly* does Beijing leverage its economic clout for regional dominance? Hugh doesn't say. In its diplomacy, Beijing is hardly looked to as the regional problem-solver; to the contrary, it's seen as a passive or sometimes disruptive actor. As for China's soft power – what soft power? Hugh does, in one sentence, allude to China's growing military power, but provides no real evidence of it. The fact is that China still possesses *no real power projection capabilities* (aside from cyber and ballistic missiles) beyond several hundred nautical miles from its shoreline. Even its navy remains more of a "green water" than "blue water" force.

Crisis Management

Hugh also alleges that the United States is not prepared to fight a war with China and would succumb early in a crisis. His essay even includes an imagined simulation of the White House Situation Room, where the President and his national command team capitulate to Beijing rather than risk a nuclear exchange. Later Hugh adds that "Washington has never acknowledged such mutual [nuclear] vulnerability with China" but "in any East Asian crisis, it is much more likely that America will back off first ... America can only be sure that a confrontation with China won't go nuclear if it is the one that backs off."

Again, this is nonsense. I certainly do not have access to the Pentagon's war plans against China, but neither does Hugh. What I do know is that it is not in America's strategic DNA to yield to an adversary like China. The US Strategic Command takes China's limited nuclear deterrent quite seriously – but the United States proceeds in crisis management from the assumption of overwhelming nuclear superiority.

Australia's Choices

Finally, Hugh's essay draws various wrongheaded policy conclusions for Australia from his flawed analysis. He starkly asserts:

> Canberra has had to decide how far it can support America without alienating Beijing, how far it can please China without risking a rebuke from Washington ... We are, most probably, soon going to find ourselves in an Asia dominated by China, where America plays little or no strategic role at all ... America is stepping away from Asia, and that means it is stepping away from us ... We are going to be on our own ... We should do what we can to build a new relationship with America – a post-alliance relationship.

Then he darkly prophesies that "Beijing could one day try to impose its brand of authoritarian politics, dictate national policies and control our economy to its advantage. At the worst, it could invade the country and subject it to direct rule from Beijing ... We can no longer afford to assume that America would come to our aid."

I am certainly not Australian, but I have visited your wonderful country numerous times and I have closely followed the debates Down Under concerning China in recent years and months. I must confess complete bewilderment at the very notion that there is even a *choice* contemplated for Australia between the United States and China, and that China somehow offers a viable and valid strategic and moral alternative to the alliance with the United States. I ask all Australians: what *values* do you really have in common with the People's Republic of China and the Chinese Communist Party? Alliances and long-term strategic partnership must be anchored by common values. How much blood have Australians and Americans spilled in combat together defending those common values? And are recent revelations of China's "influence operations" and exporting of censorship to Australia signs of value convergence? Australia can certainly have China as its primary economic partner, but do iron ore exports really equal a foreign policy? I thus find it both delusory and dangerous to argue, as Hugh does, that America is going to abandon Australia (and Asia), that Australia will find itself "on its own," and that Australians and Asians have no choice but to accommodate Chinese hegemony.

I therefore find Hugh White's essay, while highly provocative, to be profoundly incorrect in its assessments of the major players and the major trends – which leads him to prescribe equally unsound policies for Australia. Relax, Australia – America has your back, and always will. America is not about to retreat from Asia – from Teddy Roosevelt to the present and well into the future, America will be a fully engaged Indo-Pacific power. For as far as my eye can see, Asia will be the site of a strategic *contest* between the United States and China. The US–China competition is far from over – it is intensifying, across Asia and the world.

Finally, I know of no Asians who wish to live under a *Pax Sinica* – a new "tribute system" – even if China had the capabilities to extend its power over the region (which it does not). Looking to the future, the empirical reality and the principal strategic challenge for all countries in Asia is to "manage" the US–China competition and to keep it from becoming fully adversarial. Australians and other Asian states possess their own agency and should work to ameliorate the rising competition while countering Chinese assertiveness. This is what the grand strategists should be concentrating their analytical efforts on.

David Shambaugh

John Fitzgerald

People in China who follow Chinese-language news sites in Australia would have been alarmed by warnings that started flashing on their touch screens late last year. "We remind all Chinese overseas students in Australia to be wary of possible safety risks in Australia," China's embassy and consulates cautioned in an official alert on 20 December. "Attacks and insults targeting Chinese students have been taking place around Australia." The warning was repeated locally between music breaks on PRC-funded Chinese-language radio stations and websites such as Melbourne's 3CW, in endless loops, along with a recitation of phone numbers for presumably distressed students who needed to contact their local consulates.

The warning came less than a fortnight after the Chinese embassy in Canberra issued a strongly worded statement in Chinese and English condemning Australian media for "repeatedly fabricating news stories about the so-called Chinese influence and infiltration in Australia," making "unjustifiable accusations against the Chinese government" and "unscrupulously vilifying Chinese students as well as the Chinese community in Australia with racial prejudice."

As if that were not enough, Australia came in for a hiding on Chinese-language community and commercial media in Australia and on local social media platforms tied to Beijing. Popular Chinese-language digital news services, including *Queensland Today* and *Melbourne Today*, carried stories about duty-free stores in Australia singling out tourists from China to diddle them, and about the children of students who had come to Australia to study who were suiciding in despair when they found they could not fit into Australian society.

The timing of these pointed messages could have been coincidental. The conjunction of official warnings and popular bad-news stories on Beijing-friendly media in Australia offers a timely reminder, nevertheless, of the tools the Chinese government has at its disposal should it ever wish to launch a Chinese consumer boycott of Australian tourism and education. Authorities in China would only need to signal to their Australia-based consular services and PRC-friendly media platforms that it was game on, and it could well be game over for many Australian universities and regional communities.

Why would Beijing want to do such a thing?

The latest instalment in Hugh White's strategic tour de force helps explain why. *Without America* commands attention as an up-to-date elaboration of White's longstanding projections on the massive geostrategic shifts underway in our region. In this latest iteration, the contest between the United States and China for regional supremacy is over, bar the shouting. Australia has to start learning to live without America and, by implication, with China.

This is where things get interesting. On top of its geopolitical forecasts, *Without America* merits attention for probing what lies beyond American hegemony and asking what kind of state China is likely to be, how it is likely to behave, what kinds of values it is likely to profess, and what kinds of threats it could pose to Australia's own values, interests and institutions over time as we try to get along with it.

In posing these questions, the willingness White showed in earlier volumes to accede to China's demands, and make allowance for its expanding role as a regional actor, has diminished as that country's triumph looms into view. There is probably little point proposing that this or that concession should be made to China when Beijing is prepared to take whatever you are prepared to concede without bothering to ask. In *Without America*, White sensibly shifts from asking what should be conceded to China, whatever the cost, to asking what it is that Australia and other countries should not concede to China at any price.

This is the question of the moment. Rather than answer it himself, White puts the question out there for public discussion.

In fact, this is pretty close to where we are already sitting in the current national debate on Chinese-influence operations in Australia. We got here not because we were thinking about grand strategy but because China's unrelenting influence operations in Australian infrastructure, business circles, community and mainstream media, political parties, universities and community organisations have captured attention over a number of years and forced the question upon us. Australians are now being asked whether they are prepared to yield to the incremental challenges China presents to their sovereignty, integrity, cohesion and security, and invited to think about the balance they are prepared to strike between their economic interests and their sense of self-worth.

As far as foreign-influence operations are concerned, Australia is on its own. It does not matter greatly whether China has or has not won in its grand strategic competition with America. What matters is the extent of Australian dependence on Chinese markets and, should it come to that, the degree of pain Australians are prepared to endure to defend their sovereignty and integrity. Dependence on Chinese markets does not compel Australians to overlook Chinese government interference operations, but it does require them to weigh the cost of any action to put an end to them. The greater its economic dependence, the more vulnerable Australia becomes to China's political and strategic leverage.

China already has the capacity to impose heavy costs on Australia for not complying with its wishes. It is not entirely clear where China's wishes start and end, but a few of them are sufficiently well known to help clarify when and how we might be transgressing them.

Some items on China's wish list are the same as those of any great power: for example, the expectation that it should be consulted and taken into consideration in any major geostrategic developments in the region. Others are peculiar to the arcane political culture and ethno-nationalism of the Chinese Communist Party (CCP) in the post-communist era.

The party wants to harness the sixty million–strong Chinese diaspora to Xi Jinping's China Dream, irrespective of nationality, and to silence the CCP's critics among them, particularly those who publish online overseas in the Chinese language. Several of China's influence operations in Australia are framed with Chinese Australians in mind and are defended in Beijing on national security grounds, which is no trivial matter.

Others relate to the overt conduct of foreign governments, best captured in a negative wish list of what they should refrain from doing in public: not engage in official conduct that could harm the interests, the standing or the "face" of the CCP or government, not act or speak in open defiance of Chinese policy or behaviour, not challenge China's "core" interests, not collaborate with other countries in ways that might appear to threaten China's security.

Prime Minister Malcolm Turnbull's comments introducing the National Security Legislation Amendment Bill to parliament on 7 December 2017 touched on a number of these sensitivities at once. Among other things, he referred to press reports of Chinese government interference operations in Australia and indicated Australia would "stand up" to defend its sovereignty in the face of China's challenges. The speech appears to have triggered the warnings and messages issuing from China's representatives and friendly media platforms in Australia around the turn of the year.

The sombre tones of those official consular warnings broadcast over and again on Chinese community radio sounded to all appearances like a tsunami alert. But this was a cautioning of a different kind. The government of China is warning the government of Australia that it is prepared to teach Australia a lesson for stepping out of line.

And so we have a foretaste of life with China. Discussion of Beijing's "soft power" operations in Australia to date has focused on their intended impact on Australian policies and behaviours through donations towards political parties, funding for university centres, equity holdings in local community media and the like. But these investments are also about China influencing China.

Foreign messaging in the Chinese language is widely read throughout China, and local social media messaging in Australia has instant global reach. Beijing has the intent and the capacity to target WeChat readers and online audiences in China from within its Australia-based media operations. When Beijing really decides to mobilise its capacity within Australia to influence the consumer choices people make in China, Australians will have to start thinking very hard indeed about how they will live with China and still retain control over their own destiny.

We count for very little in China's grand strategy. The first lesson on living with China in a world without America is that China is all about China and not at all about us.

John Fitzgerald

Merriden Varrall

Hugh White's *Without America* is an epic exploration of how White sees the future of the region unfolding and what needs to be done about it. He is, as I often find, right about a lot of things, but his argument is predicated on a number of incorrect assumptions about China and how it sees itself and its role in the world. These assumptions matter. While some would argue that understanding the Chinese perspective is at best useless and at worst appeasement, the truth is that our disregard for China's views is in large part responsible for where we find ourselves today – with China no nearer to "us" than it was three decades ago. Indeed, it is further away, and even less inclined to take a positive view of "our" approach to regional and global norms. If we want to stand half a chance of not making further foreign policy mistakes, we need to understand China's own sense of itself.

White argues that China wants to replace the United States in the region and that now, only a major war or a very credible threat will deter it. He posits that the United States is no longer in a position to issue such a threat. When this is combined with the likely reality of Chinese regional preponderance, White concludes that the costs of a major war would be far worse than the costs of Chinese hegemony, so we'd better get used to the idea of China as the major regional power. Basically, it's too late for Australia to "choose" – the choice has been made for us. We have to work out what to do about it, and "moral panic" doesn't cut it as a policy. White is exhorting Australia to wake up to what's really happening, and to take foreign policy seriously, rather than trying to cling to an anachronistic Rudyard Kipling view of the world.

When it comes to China, White is right about a few things. For example, it is timely and important to raise the question of what China's increased role in the region might actually look like, rather than just assume it will be very bad. White argues that we should think clearly about what is at stake, and that the question we now need to consider is "what kind of threat China as the domi-nant power in East Asia would, or does, pose." Despite others arguing otherwise, White is right to conclude it is highly unlikely that China is going to impose truly oppressive hegemony on Australia. He is certainly right that we need to think a lot more about influencing China to our advantage. He makes an excellent point that we can afford to be more thick-skinned and that we are silly to exaggerate the costs we might pay for displeasing Beijing. He is also right that China does want to reshape the global economic order to serve its own economy as it grows and changes. He's right that the Chinese political elite want to protect their ideology and political system from outside influence and guarantee their territorial security. He's right that the primary goal of the governing elites is to protect the Party. He's right that they want more than what they've got in East Asia. He's right that what the US and its allies have done so far, including freedom of navigation operations, for example, hasn't made any positive difference.

However, White's analytical lens colours his understanding of what China is and how China sees the world and its own role within it. White's perspec-tive is classic international relations realism. For realists, nation-states are understood as neatly bounded geopolitical entities. They have a "will to power" as their driving motivation, and they act rationally to achieve that, weighing up costs and benefits just as any other nation-state entity in their situation would. Achieving power is a zero-sum calculation: there can be only one hegemon – as you go up, I go down, and vice versa. There is little room for perspectives, ideas, psychology, culture, plurality, multipolarity – other ways of seeing the world.

White's essay is peppered with characterisations of China based on this real-ist perspective. For example, he argues that China is serious about contesting US leadership in Asia and willing to defy Washington and risk confrontation to do so. He argues that, "The biggest mistake US policy-makers have made in deal-ing with China has been to underestimate how determined it is to replace America as East Asia's leading power." He says that China wants to overturn the US-led status quo and "build a new order centred on Beijing." He bases his argument and conclusions on the view that China wants to be the preponderant power and that, "like all preponderant powers it will be jealous of its place and eager to deter any support for a rival." He, like many others, describes China's actions in the South China Sea as the "classic power-political ploy of salami-slicing," a means of testing resolve to make US leadership look weak. He understands China's actions in any part of the region, including the way it has "extended its tactics to the East China Sea," as part of the same strategy. He believes that China calculates costs and benefits very rationally, or at least, in the same way as the United States does, using the same metrics of what constitutes winning and losing.

White's realist analysis concludes, unsurprisingly, that "power politics in Asia today suggests that China would need to be confronted with the real risk of a major war to be deterred." For him, there is no question about the China challenge. And there is no discussion of whether China's challenge looks the same from Beijing as it does from Canberra or Washington. In this characterisation, China wants to go up, so the US must come down. Therefore, from the point of view of the United States and its allies, China must not go up – that certainly seems to be how things look to many influential analysts in the United States. But is this how things look from Beijing? Was 2008 the moment Chinese leaders said, "Right, this is it America – we're getting serious about turfing you out now"? Or is that just how it seems from the perspective of an anxious hegemon and its allies?

I would argue that China does not see the region, or its role in it, or the United States' role in it in this zero-sum, us-or-you, win-or-else way. As I have argued elsewhere, there are several key "worldviews" that underpin how China sees its rise, and they add up to a very different perspective from the one Hugh White promulgates. They are: that history is destiny; that China has been and continues to be the victim of a longstanding effort by certain Western powers to keep it weak (which currently includes Japan, but not the United Kingdom, despite the United Kingdom's central role in the Opium Wars); that cultural characteristics are unchanging; and that relations among states are based on "familial," circular patterns of obligation and reciprocity. These worldviews are certainly politically constructed and deliberately maintained, but that does not mean they are not relevant.

Just as White sees events in Asia through his realist lens, so too does China have widely accepted, normative views of its natural, inevitable future. China sees the current situation as simply a moment in a vast, inevitable, inexorable movement back to how things should be, to China fulfilling its manifest destiny, which was knocked off-track in the mid-1800s with the Opium Wars. Chinese elites, and many of the broader population, believe China was taken by surprise because it had let itself become weak and complacent, overconfident in its own abilities. China has no intention of letting that happen again. From the Chinese point of view, that was an historical anomaly, and so the current shifts are nothing more than destiny righting itself, not a battle in a great power politics competition to dominate. The United States and Australia are just huffing and puffing about something they cannot actually prevent. As China sees it, the US presence as hegemon in Asia is an insulting irritation, but not something that can forestall the Middle Kingdom's inevitable resumption of its rightful role.

What I haven't mentioned so far is the Chinese perspective on "how things should be." This is because there is no grand plan for, or clear vision of, a new world order, and certainly no strategy to achieve it. Despite the five-year plans and tight controls over the economy and intellectual space, China didn't foresee, let alone orchestrate – and indeed wasn't very well prepared for – many of the things that have catapulted it to centre-stage in the last decade or so. For example, China was pleasantly surprised by how the global financial crisis of 2007–08 turned out for it. Trump's election has been another unexpected opportunity. While Chinese political elites are unnerved by Trump, they are not going to pass up the sudden opening in global governance that has emerged, even though they are not really prepared for it beyond rhetorical grandstanding, such as Xi Jinping's 2017 speech in Davos.

In China, the general view of "how things should be" goes something along the lines of the tribute system that arguably governed the region between the twelfth and seventeenth centuries. However, what that looks like, presuming it in fact existed, is not at all clear. The tribute system is generally understood to have been a stable, hierarchical system for international interaction centred in Asia, with China as the hegemon, and which relied on cultural achievement as much as hard power as the basis for supremacy and respect. The Chinese are, of course, cognisant that the world cannot function in that way now. But no, their vision of the future does not involve the United States as a central actor. Importantly, neither does it look like a world where China replaces the United States in a zero-sum, you're-out-and-we're-in overturning of the status quo. As White notes, far more effort needs to be expended in thinking about what China's increased role in the region could involve. But we need to go beyond the question of "when China replaces the United States." It is worth considering the possibility that China has no intention of replacing the US.

For China, it is about the long game – the really long game. China does not think in election cycles. It does not really even think in decades. The ultimate goal is China emerging from its "century of humiliation" and regaining its proper place (whatever that may in fact mean) on the world stage. Conflict is not a part of this vision. While most Chinese are immensely proud of China, and fully supportive of the goal of re-emergence, they also greatly value stability and peace. While it is not often publicly discussed, the turmoil of the Cultural Revolution and the hardship of the Great Leap Forward are still in living memory for many. The desire for a quiet and peaceful life is widely held and deeply shared. This is "the China Dream." The Chinese Communist Party works hard to ensure that this "rejuvenation" is seen by Chinese people as synonymous with its leadership. The Party's legitimacy depends in great part on the people of China seeing it as responsible for this re-emergence. China, under the Party, but probably under any leadership, is not interested in winning the proverbial battles and losing the war. What many in the United States and Australia consider to be "wins," times we have "put skin in the game" and shown China a thing or two, mean very little in the long run. China's apparent backdown over the Taiwan Straits in the mid-1990s is a good example. Has China relinquished any of its desire to incorporate Taiwan into One China under Beijing's rule? Not in the slightest. Has China come to respect the United States as the rightful hegemon in the region? The answer is obvious.

White concludes that China will not be deterred from its course (the form of which he misunderstands) unless it is convinced that there is a credible threat of major war. I disagree. I think China is more likely to make what will seem like concessions to – or even "wins" for – the US and its allies well before it comes to major war. But in the long run it is almost impossible to envisage anything that will deter it from its sense of its manifest destiny. China believes it will inevitably resume what it sees as its rightful role. However, while China wants the US to know its place, this does not mean the US, and everything it stands for, must be overturned. China believes time is on its side, so conflict is neither desirable nor necessary. It is happy to move sideways and pause from time to time in order to move forward. Ultimately, White is half-right. He is right that Australia must wake up to the reality of the changing world around it and take foreign policy seriously. But he is wrong about what that changing world is going to look like.

Merriden Varrall

Andrew Shearer

In the decade or so that Hugh White has been peddling variants of his "China Choice," I have frequently joined other commentators in crediting him for stimulating debate even while disagreeing with his analytical judgments and his policy prescriptions (to the extent he specifies them). It is tempting to greet *Without America* in that spirit.

To do so here would be a cop-out, however. The subject of White's latest essay – the strategic competition between the United States and China, and its implications for the regional order and Australia in particular – is too important. When someone has been writing and advocating on one topic for as long and as prominently as White, we are entitled to expect analytical rigour and useful policy recommendations. Unfortunately, *Without America* disappoints on both counts. It remains much more a gauzy adumbration than an actionable blueprint to help policy-makers navigate an increasingly challenging strategic environment.

In *Does America Need a Foreign Policy?* (2001), Henry Kissinger remarked that, "the successful conduct of foreign policy demands, above all, the intuitive ability to sense the future and thereby to master it." *Without America* is certainly an ambitious attempt to sense Asia's future. But it falls down not least because it misreads transitory events and ephemeral noise for consequential signals about the long-term direction of US policy. In an almost hypnotic chain of seriatim assertions, White's argument reaches his climactic judgment: "America will lose, and China will win. America will cease to play a major strategic role in Asia, and China will take its place as the dominant power." In White's interpretation of developments – particularly the advent of the Trump administration – America is already withdrawing from the region. Yet many of the analytical judgments leading to his sweeping conclusions have already been overtaken by events since he wrote his essay.

Under President Trump, White claims, "America seems to have abandoned the objective of resisting China's challenge in Asia" and "the trend in Washington seems clear. Trump is not committed to maintaining US leadership in Asia. He is content to see America's influence in the region wane while China's grows." As evidence for this proposition, White points to: Trump being "conciliatory and accommodating" towards China in office; the sidelining of "China hawks," a softening in US rhetoric towards China, and the new administration going "out of its way to emphasise cooperation with Beijing"; Washington no longer promoting "its own vision of Asia's future, in opposition to China's"; the South China Sea slipping down Washington's agenda; and the administration scarcely acknowledging that America faces a strategic contest with China in Asia.

Now let's consider what has actually been happening.

It's true that Trump fell for traditional Chinese diplomatic flattery when his hosts rolled out the red carpet on his premature first visit to Beijing last November and did not push hard enough on key issues. Trump also had a friendly but insubstantial summit with President Xi Jinping at Mar-a-Lago and, at least initially, Beijing believed it had established a special channel through presidential son-in-law Jared Kushner. There will continue to be issues where the two powers' interests overlap and they agree to work pragmatically together; China has acquiesced in new UN sanctions on Pyongyang, for example. But since he was elected, President Trump has in fact criticised China on a range of issues, particularly not going far enough to pressure North Korea, but also its trade practices. With the partial exception of North Korea, it is difficult to identify prominent areas of cooperation (such as climate change under the Obama administration).

On the contrary, the balance in the relationship has continued to shift further under Trump from engagement towards overt competition. Far from standing back and giving China a free hand to carve out a sphere of influence across Asia, as White asserts, the Trump administration's National Security Strategy and National Defense Strategy documents go further than any predecessor's in identifying China (along with Russia) as a revisionist power and strategic challenger. The National Security Strategy declares the failure of the bipartisan commitment to engagement that has framed the United States' China policy for several decades, and explicitly accuses China of attempting to reorder the region and erode American security and prosperity using a combination of economic coercion, military power and information warfare. The Strategy labels China "a strategic competitor using predatory economics to intimidate its neighbors while militarizing features in the South China Sea." In a significant shift, it declares inter-state strategic competition (including with China) the primary concern in US national security, formally supplanting terrorism.

White and other critics may dismiss both documents as the delusional bluster of a fading superpower, but prudence and decades of mistaken prophecies of American decline suggest it would be a mistake to ignore the administration's undertaking that the United States "will raise our competitive game to meet that challenge." So do a number of the administration's actions to date. Secretary of State Rex Tillerson has laid out the administration's vision of a "free and open Indo-Pacific" in direct response to China's regional power play. As well as moving to reverse the Obama administration's cuts to defence spending and rebuild US military readiness, the administration has resumed routine freedom of navigation patrols close to contested features in the South China Sea. The administration and Congress are starting to focus on Chinese efforts to influence domestic politics in the United States (reportedly in light of recent Australian experience).

The administration is also pushing back against Beijing's mercantile economic policies. Congress is moving to tighten US foreign investment rules to clamp down on intellectual-property theft by China. The United States Trade Representative flatly rejects China's market economy status, and trade experts are in accord that the recently announced measures against Chinese imports of solar panels are just the start of a concerted campaign using many of the trade levers Washington employed during the US–Japan trade spats of the 1980s and 1990s.

My point here is not to endorse the administration's policies. Tariffs are bad for consumers, inimical to growth, likely to trigger Chinese retaliation, and in the worst case could lead to a mutually destructive trade war. The decision to withdraw from the Trans-Pacific Partnership – once acknowledged by Hillary Clinton as a "gold standard" trade agreement – was a damaging self-inflicted wound. No one serious – senior administration officials included – would assert that the Trump administration yet has a fully developed, comprehensive Asia strategy. The "free and open Indo-Pacific" is a useful conceptual framework. It could be given real substance as the administration finally starts to fill senior Asia policy roles but for now is little more than a bumper sticker. Clear and consistent public messaging hasn't been one of President Trump's hallmarks, and he and his administration have at different times sent wildly varying signals on relations with China (not to mention on North Korea and a raft of other foreign policy issues). There are legitimate concerns about the president's temperament and command of foreign policy.

A certain amount of cognitive dissonance is therefore excusable when it comes to analysing this highly unconventional, disruptive and not infrequently dysfunctional presidency. Indeed, there are signs that the political leadership in

Beijing misread Trump too and has been thrown somewhat off-balance: recent visitors there confirm that officialdom remains in denial about the seriousness of US resolve on trade, for example. Even Bob Carr – another prominent advocate of an accommodationist policy towards China – is discombobulated. In May 2017, the former Labor foreign minister and diarist wrote a column for the *Sydney Morning Herald* trumpeting that the new American administration had stopped US freedom of navigation patrols in the South China, and that Australia would have been left "stranded" if it had conducted its own patrols as advocated by several commentators (including this writer). Carr isn't one to be daunted by facts, but even he must have been mildly embarrassed when the USS *Dewey* steamed within twelve nautical miles of Mischief Reef in the Spratly Islands the same day that his misconceived article appeared.

But this doesn't let more serious commentators off the hook, and it makes it even more important they resist the easy temptation to substitute modish indiscriminate Trump-bashing for sober assessment. Too often White's Quarterly Essay succumbs. As a result, it miscomprehends the United States, the Trump administration and the direction of US policy towards China and the region. It underestimates the United States, its trajectory, its enduring interests in the region, and the costs and risks it is prepared to bear to protect them and retain a strong – albeit not necessarily predominant – position in Asia. Moreover, the judgments in the two strategy documents cited earlier above do not represent the aberrant views of a handful of "China hawks" but reflect an increasingly broad consensus across the executive arm of the US government, both sides of Congress, the wider American foreign policy establishment and even many in the business sector.

Without America is likewise too dismissive of other major powers in the region and their potential to counterbalance China's growing power, in different combinations – as highlighted by the recent re-establishment of the Quadrilateral Security Dialogue between the United States, Japan, India and Australia. Under Prime Minister Shinzō Abe, Japan has a clear-eyed appreciation of challenges to the regional order and is stepping up its security contribution in ways few experts predicted even a decade ago. Far from the impression of brittleness White conveys, senior Japanese and American policy-makers and experts consistently tell me that the US–Japan alliance has never been stronger. Abe is serious about strengthening strategic ties with India and Australia. There may be a hedging aspect to this, but Abe's commitment to the US alliance is genuine and he clearly sees these relationships as augmenting rather than supplanting it, and contributing to a critical mass of like-minded powers capable of providing a counterbalance to China. Likewise India, whose geography and strategic interests, threat perceptions and values similarly point to continuing convergence among the region's major maritime democracies. Neither Japan nor India is likely to settle meekly for the circumscribed roles assigned to them in White's putative China-dominated Asia. Neither should Australia.

When he turns to Australia's role, White is unduly critical of Australian policy-makers. Australian regional diplomacy since 2000 has not been without blemish (and as someone closely involved in Australian foreign policy over for much of this period I should probably declare an interest). As historian Hal Brands observes in *What Good is Grand Strategy?: Power and Purpose in American Statecraft from Harry S. Truman to George W. Bush* (2014), "Devising a coherent, purposeful approach to international politics is hard enough, given the limits of human wisdom and the chaotic nature of global affairs. Implementing it can be harder still." Yet Australia's recent track record is hardly the failure White asserts. On the contrary, Australia has pursued – not without occasional departures and interruptions – a broadly effective balancing strategy, moving over time (in response to China's increasing power and assertiveness) along the spectrum from "softer" to "harder" forms of balancing. Working to encourage sustained US engagement in the region has been a centrepiece of strategy under Australian governments from both sides of politics for over seventy years, notwithstanding occasional differences of emphasis and tactics.

John Howard laid a firm strategic foundation. As early as 1996 he told the visiting US secretaries of state and defense that as the balance of power started to shift in the region, "new geopolitical forces and pressures emerge. These forces require careful channeling, management or offsetting. And we have no reason to believe that countries will start behaving radically different from how they have behaved for the past few thousand years." Alliances were "perhaps even more important in times of flux, and an alliance commitment is not a surrender of independence." More than twenty years ago, Howard saw that the coming challenge was "how can we encourage China – and if necessary constrain it – to behave in positive and co-operative ways as its international role grows." Over more than a decade in office Howard rebuilt Australia's defence capabilities (explicitly linking this to his government's economic growth agenda); strengthened the US alliance; signed Australia up to the Australia-Japan-US Trilateral Strategic Dialogue, the East Asia Summit and the first iteration of the Quadrilateral Security Dialogue; made the first moves to establish a serious bilateral strategic partnership with Japan; and committed – despite trenchant opposition from Labor and his own non-proliferation officials – to establish strategic trust with India by lifting the ban on uranium exports.

Kevin Rudd was the only prime minister during this period to pursue (at least initially) an accommodationist China policy, and it went badly. Hoping to curry favour in Beijing, Rudd withdrew Australia from the Quadrilateral Dialogue. He undermined trust in Tokyo by taking Japan to the International Court of Justice over whaling and let bilateral free trade negotiations drift. His quixotic Asia Pacific Community initiative went nowhere. And he overturned Howard's commitment to lifting the counterproductive ban on exporting uranium to India. These steps might have been defensible if they had ushered in a new golden age in Australian relations with China. On the contrary, they reached a new low when a frustrated prime minister lashed out famously about his Chinese counterparts (in rodent-related terms) at the Copenhagen climate talks. The Rudd government's 2009 Defence White Paper represented something of a course correction, flagging the need for a naval build-up in response to China. After replacing Rudd, Julia Gillard subsequently undid some of the damage with Japan, particularly when she was the first foreign leader to visit after the Fukushima disaster, and boosted the US alliance when she agreed to the US Force Posture Initiatives in Australia, but Labor continued to support the India uranium ban and drag its feet on free trade negotiations.

The Abbott government took the Howard framework as its template, initiating a comprehensive defence white paper and increased defence spending, strengthening the US alliance by contributing forces to the coalition military operation that recently defeated ISIL in Iraq and Syria, strengthening defence ties and concluding a free trade agreement with Japan, finally lifting the India uranium export ban and pursuing closer naval cooperation, hosting a leader-level meeting of the Trilateral Strategic Dialogue, and taking a firm position on Chinese moves that undermined the status quo in the East China Sea and the South China Sea. At the same time it maintained a pragmatic relationship with China, concluding the most comprehensive free trade agreement with that country of any major developed economy and signing on to Beijing's Asian Infrastructure Investment Bank (in the process deftly managing resistance from Washington and Tokyo and extracting substantial Chinese concessions to make its governance more transparent – a textbook piece of Australian diplomacy).

The Turnbull government has consolidated some of these successes. It has sustained the commitment to spending two per cent of GDP on defence, and the 2017 Foreign Policy White Paper went further than previous governments to articulate a credible framework for a continued Australian balancing strategy. During his recent visit to Tokyo, Prime Minister Turnbull announced with his counterpart Abe that the two countries are close to finalising a legal agreement that will facilitate more ambitious combined military exercises. In a forthright speech at the 2017 Shangri-la Dialogue in Singapore, Turnbull pointed to the risks to regional stability and prosperity posed by a coercive China; while it has refrained from authorising the Royal Australian Navy to conduct freedom of navigation operations, his government has spoken out consistently against China's efforts to change the status quo in the East and South China Seas. The government supported the re-establishment of the Quadrilateral Security Dialogue; it responded cautiously to China's Belt and Road Initiative; and it is legislating in response to revelations of covert Chinese influence operations in Australia. Labor under Bill Shorten's leadership has pursued broad bipartisanship on national security including the US alliance – although some Labor figures have used President Trump's unpopularity to call for a "more independent" Australian foreign policy (longstanding code on the Australian Left for weaker ties with the United States), and whether a Labor government would deliver, particularly on defence spending, remains to be seen.

Allowing for the difficulties inherent in strategic planning and implementation, the pace of change and increasing complexity in the region, and an unedifying period of instability in Australian politics, this is a pretty good track record. Many other countries can only envy the prosperity and relative security Australia enjoys today. There is always room for improvement, and White is right to warn Australians against complacency: the balancing task is becoming significantly more challenging, for some of the reasons outlined in Quarterly Essay 68. But it seems churlish not to give our political leaders, on both sides of politics, some credit.

Hugh White paints in broad, vibrantly hued brushstrokes daubed one on top of the other, like Vincent van Gogh. The result is vivid and striking but often lacks verisimilitude. What is needed now is realism, not impressionism. Australia is indisputably moving into a more difficult strategic era, which will test our policy-makers and demand steady, purposeful statecraft. But it is time to end the phony China Choice debate, which has been consistently rejected by both major political parties and has few if any adherents in Australia's national security community and among other serious commentators. We need to move beyond "admiring the problem" and bemoaning the lack of a strategy. Together, the defence and foreign policy white papers provide a sound conceptual framework. But they need to be implemented with greater vigour and urgency.

Andrew Shearer

Kim Beazley

Hugh White is one of Australia's substantial strategic thinkers. His Quarterly Essay won't damage that opinion. That is not to say I agree with all his projections or his analysis of the recent past. Power distributions are always shifting. The distant is most problematic, of course. But taking one projection of China's rise and distant American retreat and imposing it on the present is fraught. He himself alludes to rising competitors for China in the region. A straight-line projection of economic growth is useful, but ignores the complexity of political and economic circumstances. The suggestion, derived from where we stand now, of a long-term American retreat from an ability to use strategic weight in a region so vital to American interests is questionable. That irrespective of that trend we need to rethink current settings, I agree with.

Hugh sees the American retreat in embryo in what he perceives as the indecisiveness of the Pivot in Obama administration policy and the "isolationism" of the Trump campaign. I disagree with his characterisation of Obama's policies. The Pivot was one of the policy initiatives of which the president was most proud. Obama's linking into Asian preferences for multilateralism, manifested in the Trans-Pacific Partnership, has been trashed by Trump, disastrously in my view. However, since Trump has assumed office, his America First formulation has seen a reassertion of American military power in the zone. It has been accompanied by a policy on the Korean Peninsula that has brought us to the brink of war. Likewise, Trump's trade focus is likely to produce a serious argument with China and uncomfortable possibilities in American relations with South Korea and Japan. There is much food for thought for Australia here and a challenge for the way we use influence with our ally. However, an American retreat is not immediately on the cards or obvious in the future. China is taking US power and intent seriously enough to massively increase its pressure on the North Korean leader.

Hugh portrays Obama's Pivot as flaccidly pursued by his administration. Having witnessed it up close, I would disagree. That is not to say there was no miscalculation – there was. However, that was less a product of inattention than divided counsel among the pivoteers. They fell roughly into two camps: one assigned priority to the relationship with China; the other saw a broader relationship with Asia within which the bilateral relationship with China was to be situated. Obama's National Security Advisors Tom Donilan and Susan Rice sat firmly in the first camp. The State Department, particularly under Hillary Clinton, sat in the second.

Obama was with the first. However, as initiatives towards China seemed to meet with less success, Obama started to lean to the second. But even towards the end of his presidency, arguably the most important meeting on the administration's calendar was the annual Strategic and Economic Dialogue with China. The last in my time as ambassador saw 400 Chinese officials turn up in Washington. Yet though many agreements were signed, they grew less and less substantial. They faltered, in particular, on Chinese intransigence on investment policy, intellectual property protection, access to the Chinese market and cyber issues. American business, a protector of the process, gradually lost its sense of urgency.

The US attitude towards China's South China Sea claims was subsumed by this process. The bilateralists saw reacting to these claims as a nuisance. The broader Asia side saw it as an opportunity – a chance to stress to Southeast Asian nations that there was value in the American strategic presence. Neither saw the islands as a military difficulty for the US. As one official put it to me: in the unlikely and undesired event of war with China, it would take US forces half an hour to take them out.

The current phase started with an error by the Philippines, in publicly challenging Chinese fishermen in Scarborough Shoal. Previously, the Philippines had kept such actions quiet. By publicising them, they embarrassed China. The US looked at intervention but determined in the end that it would not have policy decided by a local power. Its ultimate reward has been a Philippines government leaning to China, albeit with China not progressing island creation there. Privately Obama's people told China they would not tolerate that activity.

Suffice it to say that policy failures around these issues were not a product of a retreat but of calculation. None of this reflected American underestimation of China. Far from it. Respect for China and engagement with it on global issues was an important aspect of American policy. Fear of China and a need to confront it featured heavily among Obama's critics. It did not with Obama. Nor did reticence in engaging with the region's affairs, both now and in the future. Obama never lost his respect for China. This was not a product of weakness, but of hope.

A different dynamic has been introduced by Trump. Obama's sporadic patrols in the zone have been replaced by regular ones. We found Obama's approach easier to handle, encased as it was in post–World War II American liberal internationalism. Trump has trashed that view, to our and America's detriment. We continue to support that outlook, and part of our task is to continue to hold it up to the Trump administration. It is apparent from the recently released US National Defense Strategy that the administration is rethinking its initial nationalist surge. It now seeks intense allied engagement, both diplomatically and militarily, in a technological renovation of armed forces and an effort to maintain the balances of power in our region underpinning the rules-based order.

We do need a deeper analysis of the character of our relationship with the United States. We are their ally like few others. That stems from the fact that unlike most nations, we plan for our own defence from our own resources in most likely contingencies. Since the 1980s we have taken the view that we should calculate what we require to defend our approaches ourselves. We appreciate the American guarantee to intervene militarily on our behalf but the threshold on that needs to be elevated to the highest possible level. In this sense, we are not consumers of American security. Unlike the situation with NATO or American alliances with South Korea and Japan, our circumstances do not oblige the United States to calculate the prospect of its own devastation as it aids us.

Our calculation is that what we need from the alliance is intelligence and access to first-class military capabilities. On the first, the joint facilities situated here and the product of the so-called "Five Eyes alliance" ensure high transparency for ourselves in our region. Our own capabilities are substantial but dwarfed by the value of the collective. Adding cyber and space in recent years has intensified the importance of the relationship. On equipment, we spend AU$14 million a working day in the American defence industry. The combination of Pine Gap, our over-the-horizon radar system and our array of aircraft give us the most potent air defence we have had. Almost all of this is American in origin. As the region develops its own capabilities, this will be more, not less, important.

Hugh is courageous in suggesting that in the event of regional nuclear proliferation we might need to think through our nuclear stance. We have thought that through before, in the 1960s, and during the Whitlam government we opted for the American umbrella and support for the non-proliferation regime. That is a position we should hold as long as possible, hopefully beyond my lifetime. There is no development at present to cause a rethink.

Absent major nuclear proliferation in the zone, the American umbrella holds good for us, but there are twists. We are not a "front-line" state, as China keeps pointing out to us in the South China Sea context. But unlike in the 1980s, local friends and allies *are* front-line states. The Five Power Defence arrangement with Malaysia and Singapore is with two of them. And we have looser security agreements with another, Indonesia. China is not an expansionist power in the classic sense, but it fears for its borders and this pushes it into the security zones of others. We cannot be indifferent to their situation. Absent our relationship with the US, our voice in their situation would be pretty negligible, and they know it.

Hugh is right that in the absence or diminution of the alliance we would need to contemplate a dramatic increase in defence spending. That would not be necessary, at least not in Hugh's dimensions, if the alliance were sustained. However, the changing power equation in the zone does require constant attention.

We have allowed ludicrous weaknesses to develop, which were not identified in our defence white paper. They are expensive to resolve. One is our appalling and unique failure (among members of the International Energy Agency) to maintain ninety days' worth of fuel reserves. The Bureau of Resources and Energy Economics estimates we have nineteen days of petrol, seventeen days of aviation fuel and twelve days of diesel. Military fuel reserves are not public, but a similar picture would prevail; likewise for war stocks of missiles and torpedos. To solve the first would involve expenditures of around $2 billion. A two-cents-per-litre increase in taxes on petrol would raise this amount, but it would be a substantial political bite. To solve the second the political task is easier. With so many programs under management in Defence, a spending shortfall emerges each year a few months short of the financial end – devote that to stocks of missiles and torpedoes capable of being acquired rapidly. Relying on rapid resupply by the United States in a crisis is fraught when it is challenged itself in this area.

Operationally, we need to assign first priority to the choke points in our marine approaches. There are five of them in the archipelago and around northern New Guinea. At the very least, we need to start thinking operationally about denial as concerns these approaches. Denial was a word used by Paul Dibb in his pre-1987 white paper report. We dropped it when we feared our policy being portrayed as Fortress Australia. In our current circumstances, it is essential.

Hugh is too pessimistic about where we would stand in American thinking as power shifts occur in the region. Were the changes he foresees in North Asia to occur, we would start to assume our World War II status as the "last bastion" – likely the irreducible minimum of their Western Pacific presence.

This is all very uncomfortable. Part of that discomfort relates to the way we handle China. It has become less easy to say no to China than to the United States. We have seen that a number of times recently, most notably on membership of China's international infrastructure investment bank. China liberally uses economic pressure to secure strategic gains. We cannot afford lurid partisan domestic debate on these matters. Gratuitous insults dished out as they were in late 2017 create unnecessary problems. We are right to raise objections to interference in our polity. The firmness has to be matched with civility in the way things are argued. We need to work hard to keep that liberal rules-based international order at the fore. We don't want respect for each nation's sovereignty to be undermined. We don't want the last-bastion positioning to emerge. That would reduce our strategic space. Strong and effective defence and diplomacy require the heft that comes from the alliance, but to maintain this will require great diplomatic dexterity.

Kim Beazley

Hugh White

It is possible that the core argument of *Without America* will turn out to be wrong. Instead of withdrawing strategically from Asia, as I predict, America might remain the region's leading power, or at least retain enough weight and influence to block China's ambitions to take its place. Like the great majority of Australians, I very much hope that this is what happens, because it would so plainly be the best outcome for us. But hoping for the best is not a policy. Our policy-makers have a responsibility to think clearly about the risk that things don't turn out so well, and what we should be doing about it.

How big is that risk? How likely is it that America will still be the, or even a, major power in Asia in twenty years' time? That depends, among other things, on the Asia experts in Washington who formulate and implement US policy. If America is to maintain a strong leadership role in our region, these are the people who will make it happen. There is no doubt that the vast majority of them are convinced that America can, will and must remain the leading power in Asia. But how clearly do they see what that will involve?

How well do they understand the task that America faces? How clearly do they assess China's power and resolve? How seriously have they considered what America will have to do to respond effectively? How carefully have they calculated what that would cost? How honestly have they weighed those costs against the fundamental interests and imperatives that US leadership in Asia is supposed to serve? How frankly have they explained all this to the American people? And how confident can they be, and can we be, that America's political leadership, and the American people, agree with their assumption that defeating China's challenge is worth what it will cost?

We have a useful opportunity to consider these questions, because four of the commentaries presented here come from the heart of Washington's Asia policy establishment.

Ely Ratner, Mike Green, Evan S. Medeiros, Andrew Shearer and David Shambaugh are all very serious players, and it is hard to imagine a group that better represents the state of thinking among the people in Washington whose ideas will shape America's response to China's power and ambition. What they say matters.

I appreciate it that such respected and authoritative figures have taken the trouble to respond in such detail to the essay. It shows the generous willingness to engage and debate which remains such an attractive feature of American intellectual life. It also offers us in Australia a chance to hear directly from them about how they see the task they face, and to judge for ourselves how well they understand what they are up against, and what it will require of them and of their country. And that in turn helps us understand how likely it is that they can steer America to preserve a leading role in Asia.

While there are important differences of tone and emphasis among these four commentaries, they all convey a strikingly consistent basic message. Some suggest that American policy today is just fine, others that adjustments are needed, but all agree that nothing fundamental has to change. To remain the leading power in Asia, America just has to keep on doing what it has done for so long. The nature of the task, and the demands it will make of America, will be much the same as they were back in the days when US leadership in Asia was uncontested.

This is the first major point on which we disagree. One key element of my argument about America's future in Asia is that America faces, in China, an entirely new kind of challenge, from an entirely new kind of challenger – one that is both more powerful and more resolved than any it has faced before – and that as a result the old policies and postures will no longer work. Over coming decades America will need to create a whole new policy to meet this new challenge. My Washington critics don't think China is a very serious challenger, so they don't think America has to do anything very different, or more demanding, to resist it. Indeed, under Obama, as Ely Ratner makes clear, they were not even sure that China was challenging America at all. Now they all agree that it is, in line with the new US National Security Strategy's identification of China as a rival. They just think that it will prove an easy rival to defeat.

Who is right? Much depends on how one judges China's power relative to America's. They argue that I overestimate China's power and underestimate America's. But none of them addresses the single biggest factor in this whole debate: the shift in relative economic weight in China's favour. They do not acknowledge the central, simple, brutal fact that China's economy is set to overtake America's to become the largest in the world, on any measure. Listing

America's economic strengths and China's economic weaknesses does nothing to dispel the significance of this shift.

Just how far and fast this shift is happening has been made clear in the Australian government's foreign policy white paper, published at the same time *Without America* was released. It presented a chart setting out the Treasury's estimates of the relative size of key economies in 2030, twelve years from now. It predicted that America's GDP will be $24 trillion and China's $42 trillion – not far from double America's. Of course, that prediction could be wrong, but it is very unlikely to be wrong by a large enough margin to justify Washington's complacency. It is not credible or responsible for American policy-makers to ignore the truly tectonic shift in the distribution of economic weight between America and China, the implications of that shift for their relative power, and the consequences of that for America's future in Asia.

Nor do they acknowledge that China's military capacities, though still behind America's in many ways, are far, far more potent today than they were even a decade ago, and that this has huge implications for the way a military clash with China would play out, how much it would cost America in blood and treasure, and how it could end. Nothing the Trump administration is doing to bolster US military capability will reverse this trend, or even do much to slow it.

And they do not see how far China has already changed the regional strategic landscape as its power and influence has grown. They are right to say that few, if any, countries in Asia want to live under China's shadow, but they are quite wrong to assume that China's neighbours are therefore willing to sacrifice their relationships with China to support America's ambitions to resist it.

Finally, they do not address the central question of the balance of resolve between the rivals. Each of these four commentaries reaffirms the orthodox Washington view that America is determined to preserve its leading role in Asia. None of them explores the Chinese side of this equation – the possibility that China is even more determined to take its place and become the leading power in East Asia. They fail, therefore, to engage with the key point that I tried to illuminate in the Situation Room scenario in the essay: that as the balance of power between the rivals becomes more equal, the advantage increasingly shifts to the side that has, and is seen to have, the greater resolve. And nothing my Washington critics say detracts from the simple, geographical fact that what happens in Asia matters more to China than it does to the United States. They too readily assume that they can set the tempo and intensity of the contest with China, and frame it in terms which they can win easily. The Chinese clearly have other views.

None of this necessarily means that America cannot maintain a leadership role in Asia. But it does mean that it would have to make an extraordinary effort to do so. Things have changed fundamentally since 1972, when US primacy became uncontested. Now it faces a determined contest from a rival that is far more powerful economically, and therefore strategically, than any it has ever faced before. To prevail, it would need to create a very new and different model of engagement with Asia, and accept a burden of costs and risks far greater than any it has borne in many decades. But there is no sign, from their critiques of my essay, that the key people in Washington who would have to design and develop this new policy understand the nature or the scale of the task.

And then, of course, there is Trump. My Washington critics all, in different ways, urge Australians to ignore the Trump phenomenon, and to have faith that they and people like them – the US foreign and strategic policy establishment – can corral Trump's America First instincts and persuade him, or his successors, to do what is needed to keep America strong in Asia. That seems to reflect a complacent assumption that Trump's election was a complete aberration, rather than a result of powerful and persistent currents in US national life, including in America's attitude to its role in the world. They take it for granted that Americans under Trump or his successors are willing to make the sacrifices needed to lead in Asia.

They cite the language on China as a rival in the new National Security Strategy, and Trump's willingness to travel to Asia last year. But there is no reason to think that Trump really believes what the National Security Strategy said, nor that the strategy itself embodies any serious idea of what to do about China. And the suggestion that a twelve-day presidential trip to Asia constitutes a serious demonstration of US resolve shows how little those who make this suggestion understand the scale of the task America faces – even leaving aside the fact that Trump's conduct on the trip sent precisely the opposite message. The weight of evidence suggests that Trump is as committed to his America First vision as he ever was.

That makes it very unlikely that Trump would commit himself to an effective policy in Asia, even if it were as cheap and easy as my Washington critics assume, or that he could convince Americans to support him if he did. It is even less plausible that Americans could be convinced to pay the far higher price that would really be involved. I would feel much more confident that my gloomy predictions about America's future in Asia will turn out to be wrong if my Washington critics showed more awareness of the need to persuade Americans that US national interests in Asia justify the real costs and risks of an intense strategic contest with China.

All this offers an important lesson for Australians. What my Washington critics' comments tell us is that the mainstream of the US foreign policy establishment remains in denial about the scale and seriousness of China's challenge. They ask us to trust them to manage China, and to support them in doing so. But they have no idea how to respond to it effectively, nor how to persuade American voters to support an effective response. That must, regrettably, increase the chances that the gloomy prediction embodied in the title of *Without America* turns out to be right.

Patrick Lawrence's intriguing comment strikes a very different note, and reminds us how diverse and rich the US debate on these questions is once one moves outside the policy establishment. There is much to explore here, but I'll just touch on two points. One is the key question of the nature of the US–China contest, which depends among other things, on what China wants. Patrick asks whether it is, or need be, a zero-sum game. Does China necessarily want America out of the Western Pacific, or does it just want America to "move over" and make some space for China at a top table that they might share?

I too have wondered this, and in some earlier work – my first Quarterly Essay, *Power Shift*, and my book *The China Choice* – I argued that America and China could reach a new modus vivendi, in which they shared power in East Asia. But it seemed to me unlikely that China would settle for that, rather than assert its own regional hegemony, unless America made it clear that there would be big costs and risks to China in trying to exclude America completely. That would, of course, require America to accept big costs and risks too. Back then I hoped America might find a way to do that: now I am much less sure that it can or will. Likewise, a power-sharing order in Asia could only emerge if America were willing to accept the complex give and take that it would require – instead, America could simply choose to withdraw once its own leadership became unsustainable. Alas, it seems that the latter is the case. Power-sharing takes two to tango, and I don't think America is up for it.

The second point is what this means for Australia. Patrick is quite right to detect a severe bout of stage fright over how we conduct ourselves in an Asia without America. How frightened we are was neatly shown in the government's 2017 Foreign Policy White Paper. Amid all the bureaucratic boilerplate, the key message was stark, and starkly incoherent. After acknowledging the profound shift in relative power, the force of China's ambitions and the uncertainties of America's response, the white paper nonetheless concluded that Australia could and should continue to rely on America to manage China for us and preserve the rules-based order which we depend on to shield us from China's power. Future historians will puzzle over this, but I think stage fright is the explanation. One only has to watch Malcolm Turnbull and Julie Bishop – or their Labor counterparts – tiptoe round the issue to see how scared of it they are.

My colleague Merriden Varrall has taught me a great deal about China, and the sketch she offers of the distinctive elements of the Chinese worldview is really important and helpful. I'm therefore rather relieved to find that our conclusions about what China wants are perhaps not as far apart as she may think. I do not really see myself as quite the rock-eating realist she suggests, in that I think the sources and motives of states' strategic actions are more complex than the classic realists allow. But I do think that states end up distilling the multiple forces acting within them into clear, if not always coherent, strategic agendas. And it does seem to me that, from all the complex factors that feed into it, we can see distilled in China today a perfectly clear and coherent agenda whose primary focus is to establish its strategic leadership in East Asia.

How far this amounts to an us-or-them zero-sum rivalry with America depends, among other things, on how America responds. If America's response to China's ambitions is – as the Washington establishment argues – simply to insist on the preservation of the US order, then the Beijing leadership is left with no choice but to either abandon its ambitions altogether, or to push back hard. If Beijing did not start off with a realist us-or-them agenda, Washington has pushed them towards it.

There is a broader point about the issues raised by Merriden and Patrick Lawrence concerning how we assess China's actions and motives. Those who know China well tend to focus on ways in which China is different from other countries. They see its unique culture, history and vision of itself as driving equally unique forms of international conduct. I'm sure that is true, but only up to a point. China today works as a state in a system of states, and it has little choice but to operate within that system, even as it seeks to change the way it works. I therefore think increasingly we need to recognise that China acts a lot like other states, and that it is therefore, for example, compelled to play power politics to assert its ambitions for more influence in the system just as other countries have done, because that is the way the system is built. And it seems to be very good at doing this.

What China will do with the power and influence it is winning through successful power politics is, of course, a separate but critical question. John Fitzgerald is in little doubt that it intends to throw its weight around in ways that fundamentally undermine our interests and even our sovereignty. I'm not sure it is quite that bad. Sovereignty is too slippery and emotive a concept to be much use to us here. Protecting sovereignty is seen as an absolute imperative, so when we regard any pressure from abroad concerning any national policy as an attack on our sovereignty, we have no choice but to resist that pressure, whatever the cost. But this way of thinking about sovereignty is fanciful. Countries adjust their policies under pressure from others all the time – it is what international relations is all about. Sovereignty consists in the power to choose how to respond to such pressure, not in the fact of responding at all.

So far, at least, I see no signs that China really threatens our sovereignty. What it is plainly doing – and John was among the first to draw attention to this – is putting more and more pressure on Australia to adjust our policies to suit its interests. But it remains up to how to respond. We can still decide whether to go along, or to pay the costs that China can impose should we resist. These are the choices we have to learn to make in a much more nuanced and sophisticated way than we have so far done. Events over the past few months, since *Without America* was published, do not suggest we are making much progress in learning how to do this. The Sam Dastyari affair showed how easily this really vital question can become subsumed by political point-scoring tinged with a hint of jingoism.

It is clear that Chinese influence is very real problem, but it is also clear that the government was happy late last year to use it for its own political purposes. It not only sought to embarrass Labor over Dastyari's conduct, but also to conjure threatening images of China in the hope of encouraging people to buy its argument that we can and must rely on America to shield us from it. On this point I disagree with John when he says that it doesn't matter much whether China has won its strategic contest with America. It makes all the difference. The ill-judged excesses of late last year show very plainly that we will never learn how to manage our relations with China until we understand that we will not be able to rely on America to manage them for us, because it is losing that contest.

And anyone who is inclined to see last December's events as signalling the start of a new policy of tough-minded resistance to Chinese pressure from Canberra should look at what the government has been saying this year. Visiting Tokyo in January, Malcolm Turnbull went out of his way to say nice things about Beijing, and both he and Julie Bishop very pointedly distanced themselves from the Trump administration's declaration that China is a strategic rival – even though they had said very much the same thing themselves last year. Have they caved to Chinese pressure to change their tune, or was the mere fear that such pressure might be applied enough?

Which brings us finally to Kim Beazley's generous and challenging comments. No one today has thought more deeply about the US–Australia alliance, or has more experience of how it works, and his remarks here show this to full advantage. He knows the working of the Obama administration well, and his analysis of the debates within it that determined the fate of the Pivot is compelling. But while he finds cause for encouragement in that analysis, I do not. As he tells it, the debates were won by those who believed that it was more important for America to get on well with China than to preserve its leadership role in Asia.

He paints that, in a memorable phrase, as "a product not of weakness, but of hope." But the hope was that America could have both: that it could get on well with China and retain regional strategic primacy. It was the hope that China would accept that, because it was not in the end serious about taking America's place. But that hope has been proved wrong. China is very serious about leading in East Asia, and it is powerful enough now to force America to choose one or the other. So America's predicament is a product of China's strength and America's relative weakness. It is hard to see that Kim really believes Trump makes this any better.

So I found Kim's fascinating argument doing more to support my pessimism than his optimism about America's future in Asia. He concludes by suggesting that even if my pessimism proves justified, America in retreat from Asia would still look to Australia as a "last bastion" in the Western Pacific, as it did in World War II, so that we could rely on it to look after us. But that is also, I think, too optimistic. In 1942, America needed a last bastion here because it was determined to reassert the position it had lost to Japan. An America which seeks no major strategic role in Asia needs no bastions on this side of the Pacific. And even if it did, what future would we have, as an American outpost in a Chinese-dominated East Asia? If Australia is to flourish, it has to flourish as part of our region, and we have to find a way to engage with that region, including its leading powers, on our own terms, when we no longer have a great and powerful friend to do it for us.

Hugh White

Kim Beazley was deputy prime minister of Australia from 1995 to 1996. He served as leader of the Labor Party and leader of the Opposition from 1996 to 2001 and again from 2005 to 2006. He was ambassador of Australia to the United States from 2010 to 2016 and is now national president of the Australian Institute of International Affairs.

John Fitzgerald is director of the Asia-Pacific Program for Social Investment and Philanthropy at Swinburne University of Technology. From 2008 to 2012 he was China Representative of the Ford Foundation in Beijing. His books include the award-winning *Big White Lie: Chinese Australians in White Australia* and *Awakening China*.

Michael Green served on the staff of the US National Security Council from 2001 to 2005, first as director for Asian affairs with responsibility for Japan, Korea, Australia and New Zealand, and then as special assistant to the president for national security affairs and senior director for Asia. He is a senior vice president for Asia at the Center for Strategic and International Studies in Washington, DC, director of Asian studies at Georgetown University and a non-resident fellow at the Lowy Institute.

Patrick Lawrence covered Asia for nearly thirty years, primarily for the *Far Eastern Economic Review* and the *International Herald Tribune*. He now writes columns on foreign affairs for the *Nation* and *Salon*. His most recent book is *Time No Longer: Americans After the American Century*. His website is www.patricklawrence.us.

Mark McKenna is one of Australia's leading historians. He has written several highly acclaimed books, including *From the Edge: Australia's Lost Histories*, *An Eye for Eternity: The Life of Manning Clark* and *Looking for Blackfellas' Point: An Australian History of Place*. He is professor of history at the University of Sydney.

Evan S. Medeiros served on the staff of the US National Security Council from 2009 to 2015, first as a director with responsibility for China, Taiwan and Mongolia affairs and then as special assistant to the president and senior director for Asian affairs. He is currently the managing director for Asia at Eurasia Group, a global political risk consultancy.

Ely Ratner is the Maurice R. Greenberg senior fellow in China studies at the Council on Foreign Relations. He most recently served as deputy national security adviser to Vice President Joe Biden.

David Shambaugh is the Gaston Sigur Professor of Asian Studies at the George Washington University. He has published more than thirty books and numerous articles, chapters and opinion articles about China and the international relations of Asia.

Andrew Shearer was national security adviser to Prime Ministers John Howard and Tony Abbott. He has held positions in the department of Foreign Affairs and Trade, the department of the Prime Minister and Cabinet, and the Office of National Assessments. He is a senior adviser on Asia-Pacific security at the Center for Strategic and International Studies in Washington and the C.D. Kemp Fellow at the Institute of Public Affairs.

Merriden Varrall is director of the East Asia Program at the Lowy Institute. She was previously assistant country director and senior policy adviser at the United Nations Development Programme in China.

Hugh White is the author of *The China Choice* and the Quarterly Essays *Power Shift* and *Without America*. He is professor of strategic studies at ANU and has been an intelligence analyst with the Office of National Assessments, a journalist with the *Sydney Morning Herald*, a senior adviser to Defence Minister Kim Beazley and Prime Minister Bob Hawke, and a senior official in the Department of Defence, where from 1995 to 2000 he was deputy secretary for strategy and intelligence and co-author of Australia's 2000 Defence White Paper.

Back Issues: (Prices include GST, postage and handling.)

- ☐ **QE 1** ($15.99) Robert Manne *In Denial*
- ☐ **QE 2** ($15.99) John Birmingham *Appeasing Jakarta*
- ☐ **QE 3** ($15.99) Guy Rundle *The Opportunist*
- ☐ **QE 4** ($15.99) Don Watson *Rabbit Syndrome*
- ☐ **QE 5** ($15.99) Mungo MacCallum *Girt By Sea*
- ☐ **QE 6** ($15.99) John Button *Beyond Belief*
- ☐ **QE 7** ($15.99) John Martinkus *Paradise Betrayed*
- ☐ **QE 8** ($15.99) Amanda Lohrey *Groundswell*
- ☐ **QE 9** ($15.99) Tim Flannery *Beautiful Lies*
- ☐ **QE 10** ($15.99) Gideon Haigh *Bad Company*
- ☐ **QE 11** ($15.99) Germaine Greer *Whitefella Jump Up*
- ☐ **QE 12** ($15.99) David Malouf *Made in England*
- ☐ **QE 13** ($15.99) Robert Manne with David Corlett *Sending Them Home*
- ☐ **QE 14** ($15.99) Paul McGeough *Mission Impossible*
- ☐ **QE 15** ($15.99) Margaret Simons *Latham's World*
- ☐ **QE 16** ($15.99) Raimond Gaita *Breach of Trust*
- ☐ **QE 17** ($15.99) John Hirst *'Kangaroo Court'*
- ☐ **QE 18** ($15.99) Gail Bell *The Worried Well*
- ☐ **QE 19** ($15.99) Judith Brett *Relaxed & Comfortable*
- ☐ **QE 20** ($15.99) John Birmingham *A Time for War*
- ☐ **QE 21** ($15.99) Clive Hamilton *What's Left?*
- ☐ **QE 22** ($15.99) Amanda Lohrey *Voting for Jesus*
- ☐ **QE 23** ($15.99) Inga Clendinnen *The History Question*
- ☐ **QE 24** ($15.99) Robyn Davidson *No Fixed Address*
- ☐ **QE 25** ($15.99) Peter Hartcher *Bipolar Nation*
- ☐ **QE 26** ($15.99) David Marr *His Master's Voice*
- ☐ **QE 27** ($15.99) Ian Lowe *Reaction Time*
- ☐ **QE 28** ($15.99) Judith Brett *Exit Right*
- ☐ **QE 29** ($15.99) Anne Manne *Love & Money*
- ☐ **QE 30** ($15.99) Paul Toohey *Last Drinks*
- ☐ **QE 31** ($15.99) Tim Flannery *Now or Never*
- ☐ **QE 32** ($15.99) Kate Jennings *American Revolution*
- ☐ **QE 33** ($15.99) Guy Pearse *Quarry Vision*
- ☐ **QE 34** ($15.99) Annabel Crabb *Stop at Nothing*
- ☐ **QE 35** ($15.99) Noel Pearson *Radical Hope*
- ☐ **QE 36** ($15.99) Mungo MacCallum *Australian Story*
- ☐ **QE 37** ($15.99) Waleed Aly *What's Right?*
- ☐ **QE 38** ($15.99) David Marr *Power Trip*
- ☐ **QE 39** ($15.99) Hugh White *Power Shift*
- ☐ **QE 40** ($15.99) George Megalogenis *Trivial Pursuit*
- ☐ **QE 41** ($15.99) David Malouf *The Happy Life*
- ☐ **QE 42** ($15.99) Judith Brett *Fair Share*
- ☐ **QE 43** ($15.99) Robert Manne *Bad News*
- ☐ **QE 44** ($15.99) Andrew Charlton *Man-Made World*
- ☐ **QE 45** ($15.99) Anna Krien *Us and Them*
- ☐ **QE 46** ($15.99) Laura Tingle *Great Expectations*
- ☐ **QE 47** ($15.99) David Marr *Political Animal*
- ☐ **QE 48** ($15.99) Tim Flannery *After the Future*
- ☐ **QE 49** ($15.99) Mark Latham *Not Dead Yet*
- ☐ **QE 50** ($15.99) Anna Goldsworthy *Unfinished Business*
- ☐ **QE 51** ($15.99) David Marr *The Prince*
- ☐ **QE 52** ($15.99) Linda Jaivin *Found in Translation*
- ☐ **QE 53** ($15.99) Paul Toohey *That Sinking Feeling*
- ☐ **QE 54** ($15.99) Andrew Charlton *Dragon's Tail*
- ☐ **QE 55** ($15.99) Noel Pearson *A Rightful Place*
- ☐ **QE 56** ($15.99) Guy Rundle *Clivosaurus*
- ☐ **QE 57** ($15.99) Karen Hitchcock *Dear Life*
- ☐ **QE 58** ($15.99) David Kilcullen *Blood Year*
- ☐ **QE 59** ($15.99) David Marr *Faction Man*
- ☐ **QE 60** ($15.99) Laura Tingle *Political Amnesia*
- ☐ **QE 61** ($15.99) George Megalogenis *Balancing Act*
- ☐ **QE 62** ($15.99) James Brown *Firing Line*
- ☐ **QE 63** ($15.99) Don Watson *Enemy Within*
- ☐ **QE 64** ($15.99) Stan Grant *The Australian Dream*
- ☐ **QE 65** ($22.99) David Marr *The White Queen*
- ☐ **QE 66** ($22.99) Anna Krien *The Long Goodbye*
- ☐ **QE 67** ($22.99) Benjamin Law *Moral Panic 101*
- ☐ **QE 68** ($22.99) Hugh White *Without America*

☐ I enclose a cheque/money order made out to Schwartz Publishing Pty Ltd.
☐ Please debit my credit card (Mastercard, Visa or Amex accepted).

Card No. ☐☐☐☐ ☐☐☐☐ ☐☐☐☐ ☐☐☐☐

Expiry date ___ / ___   **CCV** _____   **Amount $** _____

Cardholder's name _____   **Signature** _____

Name _____

Address _____

Email _____   **Phone** _____

Post or fax this form to: Quarterly Essay, Reply Paid 90094, Carlton VIC 3053 / Freecall: 1800 077 514
Tel: (03) 9486 0288 / Fax: (03) 9011 6106 / Email: subscribe@quarterlyessay.com
Subscribe online at **www.quarterlyessay.com**